# Integrating
# Music and Reading Instruction

by Laura J. Andrews and Patricia E. Sink

## Teaching Strategies for Upper-Elementary Grades

MENC MENC
MENC MENC The National Association for Music Education

Copyright © 2002
MENC—The National Association for Music Education
1806 Robert Fulton Drive
Reston, VA 20191

ISBN 1-56545-135-X

# Contents

149331

# Introduction

Arts integration remains a popular trend in educational practice. The arts help students develop positive attitudes toward school and the general educational curriculum. When carefully planned, arts instruction also contributes positively to students' intellectual and social development.[1] A variety of arts learning experiences may enhance students' understandings of all subject areas and facilitate transfer of learning from one subject to another. During the past four decades, using integrated music instruction to facilitate learning in other subject areas has attracted the attention of both educators and researchers. Research findings relative to nonmusic learning outcomes of integrated music instruction, however, remain disparate. Additionally, empirical evidence of the effects of integrated instruction on music learning is minimal.

The lessons in this publication were part of a 1997 doctoral study that focused on the influences of integrated reading and music instruction on fifth-grade students' reading achievement and reading attitude.[2] The study also examined the impact of integrated reading and music instruction on music achievement and music attitude. This publication is based on excerpts from the dissertation.[3] The lessons are presented here to offer ideas to elementary music and reading teachers who want to integrate music and reading instruction in the upper elementary grades.

In North Carolina, where this study was conducted, the Department of Public Instruction notes, "Educators consider reading skills to be among the most important skills that students develop."[4] The Department identifies reading, writing, speaking, listening, and viewing as communication skills that "enable learners to clarify thinking, to investigate, and to increase knowledge in all subject areas."[5] They also support the integration of teaching of communication skills with other subjects, stating that this "enhances the learner's ability to move from the known to the unknown, to identify relationships, and to make generalizations."[6]

Music experiences serve as effective rewards for elementary students' acquisition of reading and other communication skills. Classroom music experiences particularly aid students in the development of auditory discrimination skills, pronunciation of words, and expansion of vocabulary.[7] Music, therefore, may help students overcome speech problems. Speech-sound discrimination skills of learning disabled students in primary grades have been improved through pitch discrimination training.[8] Students' communication skills have been developed through the use of song lyrics as reading materials.[9] Communication skills also have been enhanced by pairing music concepts with literature and by developing listening skills through music activities.[10] Oral and nonverbal communication, creative writing, spelling, and grammar may be taught effectively using music as a motivational tool.[11]

Music instruction also has been used effectively to aid beginning readers by reinforcing their auditory and visual reception and discrimination abilities, visual sequential memory, and language reception and expression abilities.[12] Music experiences, thus, may foster the acquisition of students' basic communication skills. Integrated reading and music experiences, for example, may facilitate increased aural-visual discrimination and speech skills associated with reading and produce positive attitudes toward reading.

As a result of integrating reading and music instruction, an increase in reading achievement has not been shown as measured by standardized achievement tests of vocabulary and reading comprehension, such as the *Iowa Tests of Basic Skills.*[13] Also, although there appears to be a positive relationship between music and reading abilities, using integrated reading and music instruction to improve reading achievement has not been supported by research findings.[14] Children's enjoyment of literature, however, is enhanced by attention to music concepts and the integration of these concepts into discussions of specific stories and presentations of reading activities.[15] Additional research is necessary to determine if reading achievement increases when music experiences are integrated into the study of children's literature presented in the reading class.

For the integrated music and reading lessons presented in this publication, music experiences have been designed to facilitate students' achievements in vocabulary and reading comprehension, and to foster positive attitudes toward reading. In collaboration with a reading teacher, the music teacher/researcher developed these lessons based on selected readings, vocabulary terms, and thematic units.

The impact of reading and music integration on students' music achievements and attitudes also is a crucial concern of music educators. Recent research on music integration has not determined if students' music knowledge, skills, or attitudes are altered.[16] If the music profession is to accept the trend of integrating the arts into other subject areas, several questions relating to music development must be addressed. As a result of music integration in reading classes, do students' music knowledge and skills decrease, remain the same, or increase? Are there positive or negative effects of music integration on students' attitudes toward music learning? Answers to these general questions may provide music educators with information essential to making appropriate educational decisions regarding desirable and undesirable outcomes of integrating music instruction into other subject areas, such as reading.

## Attributes of an Integrated Curriculum
Four attributes have been identified in an integrated curriculum.[17] An integrated curriculum is *authentic.* Students are afforded learning experiences that are relevant

to life. An integrated curriculum is also *generative;* whereby, students construct meaning, gain insight, and use new knowledge. A third attribute of an integrated curriculum is that it is *integrative.* Students use higher-order thinking skills and transfer concepts across disciplines. An integrated curriculum is *iterative.* Students' experiences evolve from a "cyclical learning process that involves successive stages of problem formation, concept formation, application, evolution, reflection, celebration and modification."[18]

The meaning of integration within the language arts field is derived from those areas commonly referred to as "language arts," such as reading, writing, speaking, and listening.[19] Students' reading, writing, speaking, and listening skills can be developed outside of language arts classes. When students are afforded opportunities to learn concepts and develop skills across all content areas, they are able to acquire an integrated knowledge base that generally results in faster retrieval of information, flexible problem solving, and better concept transfer across content disciplines.[20]

## An Integrated Instructional Approach

Integrated instructional approaches "use the language and methodology from more than one discipline and focus on unifying themes, issues, problems, concepts, and experiences."[21] These models are based upon several fundamental ideas. Integrated instruction mirrors the world in which individuals live, makes learning relevant to students' personal lives, and creates connections among disciplines, adding coherence to vast amounts of information.

### Communication Skills

The reading series used in the lessons when they were initially presented— *Invitations to Literacy*[22]—was selected because it had been adopted by the school system where the study was conducted to develop communication skills stipulated by the state's standard course of study.[23] Level 5 of this series, *Explore,* is designed for students in grade five and is formatted according to thematic units that feature diverse genres of expression including personal narratives, autobiographies, poetry, historical accounts, plays, and songs. For example, selections from the unit entitled "From the Prairie to the Sea" include a personal narrative, "Along the Sante Fe Trail"; an autobiography, "Voices of the West"; a poem, "Bison"; a play, "Pecos Bill"; and a song, "Home on the Range." The general vocabulary skills, reading comprehension skills, and reading attitudes addressed within this unit include making judgments, creating questions, comparing and contrasting viewpoints, following directions, predicting outcomes, making inferences, summarizing content, and distinguishing fantasy from realism.

The unit "From the Prairie to the Sea" also features an excerpt from *Children of the Wild West,* an award-winning children's book by Russell Freedman.[24] Using this text, students learn how Native American children lived between the 1840s and 1890s. The author includes personal narratives from Native Americans who lived at that time. Photographs from the time period also depict how various tribes lived, the kinds of clothes boys and girls wore, and how children struggled with the changes that were generated by white settlement. The reading series also refers to other books written by Freedman, such as *Buffalo Hunt,*[25] *Cowboys of the Wild West,*[26] and *Indian Chiefs.*[27]

A book not included in the list of books in the reading series is *Lincoln: A Photobiography,*[28] which earned Freedman the 1988 Newbery Award. In addition to providing students with another source of information about the president, this book serves as a link to an integrated music listening activity. Aaron Copland's *Lincoln Portrait* and Freedman's *Lincoln: A Photobiography* provide students opportunities to learn about an American president through the pictorial collections and verbal descriptions of a writer and the musical statements of a composer. Through guided listening experiences, students are acquainted with characteristics of Copland's music and his artistic blending of text and sound in tribute to Abraham Lincoln. Additionally, students develop the ability to make associations between the music and the words they hear by examining the interplay between elements of music and creative writing. Words from the composition that are unfamiliar to fifth-grade students also may be used as vocabulary terms and discussed in context.

The lessons in this publication may be easily adapted for use with other basal reading series that conform to the state or district standards in use by a particular school system. Also, the lessons can serve as models for lessons on other thematic units and for other elementary grade levels. Integrated reading and music teaching and learning experiences focusing on the skills and attitudes developed within each thematic unit of the selected textbook reading series help students master communication skills. For example, an integrated reading and music instructional approach can provide students with opportunities to learn a collection of western trail songs featuring pertinent vocabulary words from selected readings. Native American culture and personal narratives also may be enhanced through the presentation and discussion of tribal songs, dances, and musical instruments. Through an integrated reading and music instructional approach students compose, create, perform, sing, move, and listen to music specifically associated with the thematic unit of study. Such experiences require students to use their musical skills and attitudes while engaged in developing reading skills and attitudes.

## Music Competency Goals

As specified by the *North Carolina Standard Course of Study,* a major purpose of general music instruction in grades four through six is to develop students' creative skills and cognitive abilities through music experiences.[29] For the study that served as the basis for *Integrating Music and Reading Instruction,* the competencies described in the *Course of Study* guided the development of the music instruction provided during students' biweekly music classes, as well as musical aspects of the integrated lessons.

## Children's Literature

Music and reading teachers may find children's literature to be a viable means to integrate reading and music. Using children's literature for instruction encourages creativity, improves listening skills, develops music skills and knowledge, and broadens students' awareness of other cultures.[30] Through children's literature, students explore musical sounds in conjunction with sounds suggested in stories, and they learn the concepts of repetition and contrast with the selection of appropriate instruments. Reading stories prepares students for enriched music listening experiences and helps them anticipate musical events based upon written stories studied in association with music.

Children's literature also provides avenues for exploring other cultures. Appropriate musical compositions and presentations enhance students' understandings of other people and places, and make more meaningful the accompanied stories. Music and reading teachers may use folk songs to accompany the study of folk tales, or instruments of the orchestra to visually and aurally accentuate concepts and ideas in children's books.[31] Through carefully planned activities and collaborative strategies, music used to enhance the study of children's literature possibly contributes to both reading and music achievements and attitudes.

In the reading classroom while studying children's literature, vocabulary terms may be associated with rhythmic patterns or defined by parody songs. The text organization and punctuation of a story may be compared and contrasted with musical forms and symbols that also provide direction or serve as a map. Listening selections, dances, and songs may be used to help students transfer conceptual learning by focusing on words, themes, people, and places common to reading and music experiences. Further research is needed to determine if the instructional integration of reading and music affects students' reading and music learning.

## Instructional Content and Strategies

Once you have decided to build an integrated unit of study, it is important to allow adequate time for collaboration between the participating teachers to identify integrated teaching content and strategies. The development of the integrated lessons in this publication was based upon a review of the selected basal textbook reading series,[32] children's literature selected by the classroom reading teacher (see Selected Resources), and an analysis of communication skills and music competency goals stipulated by the state's Department of Public Instruction.[33]

Also, the development of the lessons was based on research supporting the idea that an integrated teaching approach may facilitate learning transfer across music and language arts disciplines,[34] afford students opportunities to develop positive feelings toward reading and music, and broaden their knowledge across these content areas.[35] Integrated reading and music instruction was directed toward enhancing student enjoyment and understanding of children's literature by attention to reading and music concepts during learning experiences.[36]

The music teacher/researcher presented integrated reading and music activities during a twenty-minute segment of the students' reading class two times per week. She also provided music instruction during the biweekly music classes to insure a constancy in students' music learning experiences during the research study.

The integrated activities were designed to: (a) enhance students' understanding of emphasized reading and music concepts and skills, including making comparisons and contrasts, understanding text organization, and identifying musical forms; (b) afford students opportunities to learn reading and music concepts by reading, discussing, singing, listening, performing, and creating; and (c) reflect the social, cultural, and historical significance of the literature students were studying. Selected goals and objectives of integrated reading and music instruction were incorporated in lesson plans, instructional presentations, and student evaluations. After each integrated reading and music lesson, the teachers met to determine necessary modifications of integrated lessons.

Each lesson in this book identifies a selection of related standards from the National Standards for Music Education, which are part of the National Standards for Arts Education.[37] This material has been added to the original lessons to serve as a guide for teachers who are building curriculum based upon the National Standards or state music standards that are based on them. In using this book, keep in mind that the content suggested by the National Standards, like that of the lessons in this book, can be extended to be used in developmentally appropriate ways at various levels.

The study on which this book is based revealed that integrated instruction positively affected fifth-grade students' music attitudes and that the students maintained more positive reading attitudes than those with nonintegrated instruction. Additionally, fifth-grade students' reading and music achievements did not decrease when music learning was integrated into the reading classroom. More research investigating the effects of integrated reading and music instruction is needed. Developing measures of music achievement and attitude that can be used in integrated and nonintegrated learning environments is warranted. Also, research examining effects of different integrated instructional models is essential. Developing and applying integrated teaching strategies, examining and refining integrated content, and assessing student learning within and outside of the integrated classroom are promising avenues for research.

## Notes

1.  J. Hanshumaker, "The Effects of Music and Other Arts Instruction on Reading and Math Achievement and on General School Performance," *Update: Applications of Research in Music Education* 4 (1986), 10–11.

2.  Laura Jean Andrews, "Effects of an Integrated Reading and Music Instructional Approach on Fifth-Grade Students' Reading Achievement, Reading Attitude, Music Achievement, and Music Attitude," Ph.D. diss., The University of North Carolina at Greensboro, 1997.

3.  Ibid.

4.  North Carolina Department of Public Instruction, *North Carolina Standard Course of Study: An Introduction to the Competency-Based Curriculum* (Raleigh, NC: State Board of Education, 1995).

5.  Ibid.

6.  Ibid.

7.  D. McDonald, "Music and Reading Readiness," *Language Arts* 52 (1975), 872; and J. P. Turnipseed, "The Effect of Participation in Structured Classical Music Education Program on the Total Development of First-Grade Children," paper presented at the Mid-South Educational Research Conference, 1976.

8.  B. L. Baxley, "The Effects of Training in Discrimination of Pitches on the Ability to Discriminate Speech Sounds in Primary Age Children Classified as Learning Disabled in the Area of Auditory Discrimination," paper presented at the Annual International Convention, Council for Exceptional Children, 1979.

9.  A. F. Cardarelli, "Twenty-one Ways to Use Music in Teaching the Language Arts," guide prepared at Indiana State University, Evansville, IN, 1979; H. Klink, "Words and Music," *Language Arts* 53 (1976), 401–403; and S. D. Newsom, "Rock 'n Roll 'n Reading," *Journal of Reading* 22 (1979), 726–30.

10. S. G. Wright, "Music, Songs, and Literature," paper presented at the annual meeting of the National Council of Teachers of English, 1979.

11. G. C. Taylor, "Music in Language Arts Instruction," *Language Arts* 58 (1981), 363–67; and S. G. Wright, "Music: A Vehicle for Teaching Certain Aspects of the Elementary Language Arts," paper presented at the annual meeting of the National Council of Teachers of English, 1977.

12. M. J. Lloyd, "Teach Music to Aid Beginning Readers," *Reading Teacher* 32 (1978), 323–27.

13. *Iowa Tests of Basic Skills* (Itasca, Illinois: The Riverside Publishing Company, 1993).

14. E. P. Sullivan, "Using Music to Teach Reading: State of the Art Review," paper presented at the annual meeting of the National Reading Conference, 1979.

15. Wright, "Music, Songs, and Literature."

16. C. M. Colwell, "Therapeutic Applications of Music in the Whole Language Kindergarten," *Journal of Music Therapy* 31 (1994), 238–47; Thomas W. Tunks, "The Transfer of Music Learning," in *Handbook of Research on Music Teaching and Learning,* edited by Richard Colwell, 437–47 (New York: Schirmer, 1992); and Darrel L. Walters, "Sequencing for Effective Learning," in *Handbook of Research on Music Teaching and Learning,* 535–45.

17. M. Hughes, *Curriculum Integration in the Primary Grades: A Framework for Excellence* (Alexandria, VA: Association of Supervision and Curriculum Development, 1991).

18. Hughes, 11.125.

19. B. A. Busching and S. W. Lundsteen, "Curriculum Models for Integrating the Language Arts," in *Integrating the Language Arts in the Elementary School,* edited by B. A. Busching and J. I. Schwartz, 3–27 (Urbana, IL: National Council of Teachers of English, 1983); and S. Walmsley and T. Walp, "Toward an Integrated Language Arts Curriculum in Elementary School: Philosophy, Practice, and Implications," *The Elementary School Journal* 90 (1990), 251–74.

20. R. J. Spiro, W. P. Vispoel, A. S. Schmitz, and A. E. Boerger, "Knowledge Acquisition for Application: Cognitive Flexibility and Transfer in Complex Content Domains," in *Executive Control and Processes in Reading,* edited by B. K. Britton and S. M. Glynn, 177–97 (Mahwah, NJ: Erlbaum, 1987).

21. North Carolina Department of Public Instruction, 4.

22. J. D. Cooper and John J. Pikulski, ed., *Invitations to Literacy: Level 5, Explore* (Boston: Houghton Mifflin, 1996).

23. North Carolina Department of Public Instruction.

24. Russell Freedman, *Children of the Wild West* (New York: Clarion Books, 1983).

25. Russell Freedman, *Buffalo Hunt* (New York: Holiday House, 1988).

26. Russell Freedman, *Cowboys of the Wild West* (New York: Clarion Books, 1985).

27. Russell Freedman, *Indian Chiefs* (New York: Holiday House, 1987).

28. Russell Freedman, *Lincoln: A Photobiography* (New York: Clarion Books, 1987).

29. North Carolina Department of Public Instruction.

30. Jana R. Fallin, "Children's Literature as a Springboard for Music," *Music Educators Journal,* 81 (March 1995), 24–27.

31. Ibid.

32. Cooper and Pikulski.

33. North Carolina Department of Public Instruction.

34. Hanshumaker; McDonald; and E. P. Sullivan, "Using Music to Teach Reading: State of the Art Review," paper presented at the annual meeting of the National Reading Conference, 1979.

35. J. L. Miccinati, J. B. Sanford, and G. Hepner, "Teaching Reading through the Arts: An Annotated Bibliography," *Reading Teacher* 36 (1983), 412–17.

36. Wright, "Music, Songs, and Literature."

37. Consortium of National Arts Education Associations, *National Standards for Arts Education: What Every Young American Should Know and Be Able to Do* (Reston, VA: Music Educators National Conference, 1994).

# Integrated
# Lessons

Each of the lesson plans in this section includes the following: lesson focus, related standards from the National Standards for Music Education, materials, introduction, process, and summary. Text in quotation marks indicates the teacher speaking. Parentheses indicate student responses. The content of transparencies listed under Materials can be found in boxes within the lessons. Visuals listed under Materials also appear within the lessons.

# Lesson 1

## Introduction

"Good morning! I understand that you are beginning a unit on "The Sante Fe Trail" in your reading class. I have borrowed some vocabulary words from your reading textbook to create a poem that I will share with you. Let's look at each phrase of the poem together."

## Process

Display the first phrase strip. "The first phrase has a word that is underlined. What word is underlined?" (caravans) "Is caravan a vocabulary word?" (yes) "What does it mean?" (a group of wagons traveling together) "Good! Would you read this strip with me?"

<u>**Caravans**</u> **of Conestogas,**

Display the second phrase strip. "Read the second strip silently. What word is underlined?" (wallows) "Is it a vocabulary word?" (yes) "What does it mean?" (a puddle made by animals that wallow in the mud) "What animals are responsible for making the wallow in the poem?" (buffalos) "Let's read this strip together."

**Wallows made by buffalo,**

Display the third phrase strip. "What is the underlined word in this strip?" (vast) "What does vast mean?" (very large) "Let's read this strip together."

**Open prairie, vast and spacious,**

Display the fourth phrase strip. "The last strip! What word needs to be defined?" (mesa) "What is a mesa?" (a high area of land) "Good. From reading this phrase, which direction are we asked to look, up or down?" (down) "Let's read this strip together."

**From a mesa, look below.**

"I'm going to step away from this, and I want you to read this to yourself. What do the first and third phrases have in common?" Students read silently. "What do you notice, in particular, about the second and fourth lines?" (they rhyme) "We have a poem that rhymes!"

"We are going to look at this poem rhythmically. Reading it rhythmically makes it more interesting. Before we begin, let's read it as though we were reading it in a book." Read the poem with class without stressing a pulse.

Display the first strip of rhythmic notation.

"You know this is the first strip in our poem because … ?" (the meter signature appears at the left) "What kind of notes are these?" (eighth notes) "Good. Let's clap this pattern together." Provide preparatory count for simple quadruple meter. Clap the pattern with students. "Does this rhythmic pattern fit 'Caravans of Conestogas'?" (yes)

Display the second strip of rhythmic notation.

"Let's read the second strip of words and clap the rhythm of the words." Provide preparatory count for simple quadruple meter. Clap and chant the words with the class. "This pattern is almost identical to the first. What is different about the second pattern?" (it ends with a quarter note rather than two eighths)

Display the third strip of rhythmic notation.

"Clap with me the third strip of words while I read them aloud." Provide preparatory count for simple quadruple meter. "What pattern strip is identical to 'open prairie, vast and spacious'?" (the first strip of notation) "Are you discovering a form? If we label our first strip of notation 'A' and our second strip 'B,' because its pattern is different from the first, what would we label the third strip?" (A) "Yes! We are jammin'!"

Display the fourth strip of rhythmic notation.

Provide preparatory count for simple quadruple meter. Clap the rhythmic pattern with the class.

"This last pattern is the same as … ?" (the second rhythmic pattern) "Great!"

"The four patterns we have clapped fit the rhythm of the words to our poem. Let's tap the rhythm of the words on an open palm so that the tapping does not overpower our chanting of the poem. Are you ready to read the entire poem?" Provide preparatory count for simple quadruple meter. Clap and chant the poem with the class. "Excellent!"

"I understand that you are keeping a reading journal. Are you writing about daily experiences as if you had lived during the 1800s? Here is my sentence from my journal!"

Display sentence strip.

**I am tired.**

"How many syllables do you hear in this sentence?" (three) "How many notes are needed to fit this three-syllable pattern?" (three) "If I am writing in a meter of 4/4, and my three notes are quarter notes, what must I have at the end of the sentence to fill the fourth beat?" (a rest)

Display the strip showing three quarter notes followed by a quarter rest.

Clap the pattern with the class.

"Here is the second sentence from my journal. I thought this sentence should explain why I am tired."

Display the second sentence strip.

**We have traveled many miles.**

Provide time for students to read the sentence silently. Ask students to think of a rhythmic pattern for this sentence. Clap the rhythm of the words while saying this sentence with the class. Display the strip showing six eighth notes followed by one quarter note.

Clap the pattern with the class.

"Please take an index card and put your name at the top. When you have signed your card, look up at me."

Display a new strip of rhythmic notation.

"Look at this new strip and tap it silently in your head. Let's clap it together now." Provide preparatory count for simple quadruple meter. Clap the pattern with the class.

"I would like you to compose one sentence for me that will fit this rhythmic pattern. Make sure that your sentence is appropriate for your reading journal; remember that you are traveling along the Sante Fe Trail in the 1800s. How many syllables are in this pattern?" (five) "How many beats are in this pattern? (four) Double-check your pattern and be sure your name is on your card. We will check these next week."

## Summary

"Today we practiced reading rhythmic notation using vocabulary words from your reading textbook. We discovered that our poem was made up of some phrases that were the same and some that were different. We were able to identify a form from looking at the phrases. What was the form of our poem?" (ABAB) "We also composed our own sentences using a new rhythmic pattern. Great job today. See you next time!"

# Lesson 2

## Focus
- Reading rhythmic patterns incorporating vocabulary words
- Listening to programmatic music
- Writing creative descriptions of a musical example

## Related National Music Standards
- Grades K–4—Standards 5a, 6b, 8b
- Grades 5–8—Standards 5a, 6a, 8b

## Materials
- Visuals—four rhythmic patterns, written on the board; and list of vocabulary words, written to one side of the rhythmic patterns on the board
- Recording of "Sunrise," from *Grand Canyon Suite,* by Grofé
- *Invitations to Literacy: Level 5, Explore* (Boston: Houghton Mifflin, 1996); or excerpt from another reading text about life along the Sante Fe Trail
- Audio-playback equipment
- Pencils

## Introduction

"**G**ood morning! You fill in the missing words! 'Caravans of Conestogas, wallows made by (buffalo), open prairie, vast and spacious, from a mesa, (look below).' Remember the rhythmic patterns we practiced last week? You have remembered the words we used!"

## Process

"Today I have brought a few more patterns." Display four rhythmic patterns on the board.

Display the list of vocabulary words, written to one side of the rhythmic patterns.

roadrunners
dashboard
caravans
desolate
Sante Fe Trail

Direct students to look at the terms and match each term with the corresponding rhythmic pattern. "Which pattern fits the word 'roadrunners'?" (pattern 1) "That is correct. Everyone speak the word in rhythm with me." Provide preparatory count in simple quadruple meter. Say the word with the class. "What rhythmic syllables do we use in music class to speak this pattern?" (ta ti-ti) "Which pattern matches the word 'dashboard'?" (pattern 4) "Let's speak this word in rhythm." Provide preparatory count. Say the word with the class. "What rhythmic syllables do we use to speak this in music class?" (ta ta) "Which pattern matches the term 'caravans'?" (pattern 2) "Let's speak the rhythm of 'caravans' together." Provide preparatory count. Say the word with the class. "What rhythmic syllables do we use in music class to speak this pattern?" (ti-ti ta) "Which pattern belongs with the word 'desolate'?" (pattern 2) "Let's speak this word in rhythm." Provide preparatory count. Say the word with the class.

"Are the rhythmic syllables we use in music class the same for 'caravans' and 'desolate'?" (yes) "The third pattern on the board matches what words?" (Sante Fe Trail) "Everyone clap that pattern and say 'Sante Fe Trail' with me." Provide preparatory count. Say the words with the class.

Direct students to open their reading textbooks to page 450. Ask a student to read aloud the first full paragraph on the page, beginning with "Captain Aubry told us … " "Please read along silently in your book while [name of student] reads aloud." Student reads aloud. "From this reading, do you think Captain Aubry likes New Mexico?" (yes) "Can living in New Mexico be dangerous?" (yes) "Exciting?" (yes)

"I would like you to listen to a piece of music. As you listen, imagine that you are sitting in a Conestoga wagon, traveling with your family on the Sante Fe Trail. I want your interpretation of what is happening on the trail; there is no right or wrong answer to this activity. You may write words, sentences, paragraphs, or even an essay if you choose. But let the music guide you. What is happening in the music to create your image?"

Play the recording of "Sunrise," from *Grand Canyon Suite,* by Grofé. Monitor the class while they listen.

"Who would like to share with the class his or her description of the trail?" Provide students with opportunities to share their responses. "What about the music helped you decide that birds were chirping?" (short, high sounds of the flute) "Some of you imagined a buffalo stampede was taking place. What in the music helped to create this scene for you?" (the music became louder; more instruments were playing; the music became faster) "Why did some of you believe that you had reached your destination at the end of the piece?" (the music sounded happy; the music climbed higher; the music was very loud)

"Thank you for listening closely and for such great writing examples! I want to tell you what this music is really about. This piece is not about the Sante Fe Trail, but it does describe a national landmark in a Southwestern state. The state is Arizona. Can you tell me what national park is located in that state?" (the Grand Canyon) "The music you heard today comes from a work called the *Grand Canyon Suite*. "We listened to a movement of this suite called 'Sunrise.' The composer of this piece must have been thinking about a morning in the Grand Canyon when he wrote this movement."

## Summary
"Great work today! We practiced reading more rhythmic patterns and pairing them with vocabulary terms that you are learning. What was the name of the piece we listened to?" ("Sunrise," from *Grand Canyon Suite*) "You may put your reading textbook and pencil away. Thanks for listening so closely. I can't wait to read your Sante Fe Trail stories. Have a good day!"

# Lesson 3

**Focus**
- Listening to music of the Navajo and Zuni tribes
- Listening to and reading about the Native American flute

**Related National Music Standards**
- Grades K–4—Standards 6b, 8b, 9a
- Grades 5–8—Standards 8b, 9a

**Materials**
- Recording of "Lonely Is the Hogan," in *World of Music*, Grade 5 (Parsippany, NJ: Silver Burdett Ginn, 1988, 1991)
- Recording of "Zuni Sunrise Call," in *The Music Connection*, Grade 5 (Parsippany, NJ: Silver Burdett Ginn, 1995); or *Making Music*, Grade 5 (Glenview, IL: Silver Burdett/Scott Foresman, 2002).
- Recording of "Zuni Song," in *The Music Connection*, Grade 5
- Transparency—Native American Flute
- Audio-playback equipment
- Overhead projector

## Introduction

"Greetings! I have been reading your stories from last week. Do you remember how we wrote our stories? We listened for ideas in a piece of music. What time of day was the composer of *Grand Canyon Suite* describing?" (morning) "Yes." Share student responses with the class. "What did I really want you to focus on?" (how we felt as pioneers in the 1800s; how the music helped us with ideas) "I am impressed with your creativity and originality!"

"This week as you begin reading the autobiography 'Voices of the West' in your reading textbooks, you will be coming across new words that will have to do with where people lived. These people may have been settlers or frontiersmen, or Native Americans. Some of the words I will be discussing today pertain to Native American life."

## Process

"How many of you recognize the word *tipi*? What is a tipi?" (a type of Native American home) "Yes. Another word that I will use today is the word *hogan*." Ask a student to read the definition for hogan in the dictionary. Student reads definition aloud to the class. "Thank you. So a hogan is a home constructed from dirt and logs and built primarily by the Navajo tribe."

"We are going to listen to a Navajo song called, 'Lonely Is the Hogan.' We now know that a hogan is a Native American home. I want you to listen for a vocabulary word we discussed last week that is used in this song. I also want you to tell me what season is the subject of this song."

Play the recording of "Lonely Is the Hogan." "What vocabulary word was used in this song?" (mesa) "Good. What is a mesa?" (a high, flat area of land) "Why is the sod house lonely?" (It is winter.) "Good!"

"Without hearing the song again, can anyone tell me what two instruments you heard being played?" (a drum and a flute) "Yes. The flute that we heard in this song is not the flute we see in a marching band or symphony orchestra. We just heard a Native American flute carved from wood and likely to be beautifully designed."

"The drum was playing the same rhythmic pattern over and over. We have discussed the term used to describe a repeated pattern in music class. Who remembers what that term is? The term begins with the letter 'o.' " (an ostinato) "Yes!"

"In studying the Sante Fe Trail, what states did we learn that pioneers would cross as they traveled?" (Oklahoma, Arizona, and New Mexico) "We are going to hear a song sung by a Native American tribe of New Mexico. They are members of the Zuni tribe." Write "Zuni" on the board. "These Native Americans lived in western New Mexico. Before we listen, may I have someone volunteer to read about the Native American flute?"

Display the transparency of Native American Flute. Direct a student to read from the screen as the class follows silently.

### Native American Flute

Among the Zuni, the Navajo, and numerous other Native American groups, the flute is popular. It is viewed as "the breath of life" and is played for courtship, for reflection, and for many ceremonial gatherings. It is similar to a recorder, with a blockage near the mouth, and may have from three to six finger holes. Flutes are made from cane (a light, hollowed-out stalk of a plant), clay, wood, or bone. Some are ornately decorated with notches, paints, or hanging pieces of leather and beads.

"Excellent job! I have some underlined words in this passage. The first one is … ?" (Navajo) "You may also find 'Navajo' spelled 'N-a-v-a-h-o.' Both spellings refer to one tribe. From this passage, do you think that the flute is an important instrument to Navajo people?" (yes) "Why do you suppose Navajos refer to the flute as the 'breath of life'?" Guide students to understanding the significance of instruments, animals, and everything from the earth to the Native American way of life. "The flute is used for 'ceremonial' gatherings. What does ceremonial mean?" Guide students to understanding Native American ceremonies and the role of music in them. "Is the Native American flute similar to our recorder? In what ways?" Explain to students that recorders originally were carved from wood. "Wooden recorders are still made today, but we are accustomed to playing plastic recorders at school."

"The flute is also ornately decorated. What does 'ornately' mean? Think of the word 'ornament' that we hear often during the Christmas holiday. How do you suppose the flute looks, plain or very beautiful?" (very beautiful)

"This is another piece of music that features the Native American flute. Listen to the tone of this flute." Play the recording of "Zuni Song." "Does this music sound joyous in mood or solemn?" (solemn) "What about the flute's melody makes it sound solemn?" (the music moves slowly; phrases are long; the melody is played softly) "Did you hear any other instruments playing?" (no)

"One last piece I want you to hear is the 'Zuni Sunrise Call.' Last week you will remember that we listened to another piece about the sunrise. Remember the movement from *Grand Canyon Suite?* Let's listen now to a Native American piece about the sunrise. This song is performed on the Native American flute. You will hear a Native American man singing, too." Play the recording of "Zuni Sunrise Call."

"Do you notice something about the beginning and the ending of this piece?" (the flute played at the beginning and at the end) "Was the singer accompanied by the flute?" (no)

## Summary
"Which tribe do we associate with the word 'hogan'?" (Navajo) "Which tribe do we associate with the area of western New Mexico?" (Zuni) "Do Native American tribes value music in their culture?" (yes) "Is music used for ceremonial gatherings as well as being a part of daily life?" (yes) "What are two instruments used by Native Americans in their musical performances?" (flute and drum)

"As you read more about Native American culture this week, remember words like 'hogan' and 'Navajo' and 'Zuni,' and remember the music we heard belonging to these two particular tribes. Have a good day!"

# Lesson 4

## Focus
- Listening to Native American dances
- Reading a poem expressively

## Related National Music Standards
- Grades K–4—Standards 6a, 6b, 8a, 8b, 9b
- Grades 5–8—Standards 6b, 8b, 9a

## Materials
- Recording of "Buffalo Dance Song," in *The Music Connection*, Grade 2 (Parsippany, NJ: Silver Burdett Ginn, 1995)
- Recording of "Bear Dance Song," in *The Music Connection*, Grade 3
- Transparency—Native American Dances
- "Bison," poem in *Invitations to Literacy: Level 5, Explore* (Boston: Houghton Mifflin, 1996); or another appropriate Native American poem
- excerpt from *The Story of the Oregon Trail*, by R. Conrad Stein (Children's Press, 1984) —see Process
- Audio-playback equipment
- Overhead projector

## Introduction

"Good morning! Who remembers what two Native American tribes we discussed last time?" (Navajo and Zuni) "Good! What piece did we listen to last week that we associate with the Zuni people?" (the "Zuni Sunrise Song") "Yes! You remembered! What two sounds did we hear in this piece?" (flute and voice) "What instruments did we hear in 'Lonely Is the Hogan'?" (flute and drum) "What is a hogan?" (a Navajo home made of dirt and logs)

"What do you remember about the flute? Was it delicately carved and ornately decorated?" (yes) "Was it important in Native American culture?" (yes) "Today we are going to hear Native American dance music."

## Process
Display the transparency of Native American Dances. Ask a student to read aloud while the class follows silently.

"Thank you for reading. Some of you have probably seen a buffalo dance performed if you visited a reservation. Today, we will hear two dances. The first is a buffalo dance, and the second is called a bear dance. When you are listening to the buffalo dance, I want you to listen for the form of this piece. We have talked about form in music class. Let me know if you hear portions that repeat. Let me know if you hear parts that sound the same or parts that sound different. We will pause between the buffalo dance and the bear dance and discuss what you heard."

Play the recording of "Buffalo Dance Song."

"Who can tell me something about 'Buffalo Dance Song'?" (someone was jingling bells) "Yes, bells were probably a part of the dancer's costume. What other sounds did you hear?" (drums) "Yes. Drums established a pulse. What did you notice about the pulse as the dance progressed?" (the beat became faster at times and slower at others) "Did you hear sections of the dance repeated?" (yes) "How many different sections did you hear?" (two) "Good! How did the tempo of the dance help you in determining the form?" (it changed; one section was faster than the other) "Yes! Did you hear one person singing or a group of singers?" (a group of singers) "Did you hear men or women singing?" (men) "Who hunted the buffalo, men or women?" (men)

"Let's listen to the next piece, 'Bear Dance Song.' Listen for special effects in this dance. I don't mean effects like those you hear in movie soundtracks. Listen for instrumental sounds that occur throughout the dance. Try to determine the sound source and what you believe the sound represents. Here we go!"

Play the recording of "Bear Dance Song."

"What special effect did you hear?" (some instrument that sounded like it was scraping against something) "Yes. It sounds like something wooden, doesn't it?" (yes) "Could it be a gourd?" (yes) "What animal do you think this instrument is suggesting?" (a bear) "And what do you think the bear is doing according to the sound of the instrument?" (The bear is growling.)

"Good! Animals are sacred to Native American culture. You will learn more about this in your reading this week and in your study of Native American life in the West."

"Today we have heard two Native American dances that pay homage to the bear and the buffalo. Do you believe these animals hold a particular place in Native American culture?" (yes)

> ## Native American Dances
> Native Americans have often developed dances based upon movements of animals and movements of people who hunted animals. The "Buffalo Dance" was performed by tribesmen before they went hunting.
>
> The "Bear Dance" was popular among the Utes in Southwest Colorado and Northwest Utah. This dance honors the bear, a symbol of power. Dancers often wear a bear skin and even a bear head as a costume.

"Did you notice what the instrument began to play while the vocal section was performed in 'Bear Dance Song'? What was the 'growling' instrument keeping?" (the steady beat) "You had to listen very carefully because the instrument was played softly in the background during the vocal section. Good listening!"

"Let's look at the poem 'Bison' on page 470 in your reading textbooks. I heard you reading from this page earlier in your reading class." Ask for student volunteers to read the poem. Direct student volunteers to read assigned sections. Ask the class to follow along silently in their textbooks.

"Thank you, readers! Everyone look at the first line in the poem. Is that a declarative statement or a question?" (a question) "Let's look at this question and imagine how it would sound if we were a Native American walking the Great Plains, searching everywhere for buffalo. Let's imagine, too, that we have been looking for many days because we are hungry and cold and tired. On a meadow where thousands of buffalo roamed, we cannot find one. Let's ask that question again." Read aloud with class the opening question.

"Where in the poem do you believe the author's idea is most dramatic? What statement do you feel carries the most convincing message? Here is a poem to honor an animal that keeps the Native American alive and provides so many valuable things to him. Read through the poem silently and find a statement that indicates action."

"What has the Native American done?" (He has looked for the buffalo.) Read these lines to the class. "How do you think this person feels?" (sad) "Yes!"

"We have talked about dynamics in music class. What are dynamics?" (the "louds" and "softs" in the music) "Good. Do you think this poem has 'louds' and 'softs'? Do you think the person in this poem expresses every thought with the same emotion? Remember how we asked the opening question? How do you suppose the last statement could be said? Angrily? Desperately? Perhaps solemnly, even mournfully?" (Yes. He knows he cannot live without the buffalo.)

"Your reading teacher has been reading a book titled *The Story of the Oregon Trail*. I found one passage from it particularly exciting, and I want to share it with you. Listen and see if you can tell me why I am so happy with this excerpt." Read the following brief excerpt:

> When darkness crept over the camp, Applegate wrote, "Before a tent near the river a violin makes music, and some youths and maidens have improvised a dance upon the green. In another quarter a flute gives its mellow and melancholy notes to the still air." But the music ceased and fires were doused early. Morning would come soon, and the emigrants had to face another long day on the Oregon Trail. (p. 22)

"When I read this, I jumped for joy! Why?" (Instruments were played and people danced to music.) "Yes! And someone was thoughtful enough to mention it in their journal! An actual event that took place in the evenings around camp! Music!"

## Summary

"Was music important to frontier life?" (yes) "Do you think music offered them a sense of enjoyment?" (yes) "A sense of peace?" (yes) "A sense of happiness?" (yes) "And we have learned how important it is to the Native American culture, too. Music played an important role in the lives of these people!"

"Good job! You may put your textbooks away. See you next time!"

# Lesson 5

**Focus**
- Performing a chant using rhythmic patterns based upon vocabulary words
- Reading about music as part of culture and civilization

**Related National Music Standards**
- Grades K–4—Standard 5a, 8b, 9d
- Grades 5–8—Standards 5a, 8b

**Materials**
- Transparencies—Vocabulary Words and Questions; and "Tribal Chant"
- *Invitations to Literacy: Level 5, Explore* (Boston: Houghton Mifflin, 1996); or excerpt from another reading text describing the teaching of traditional myths, songs, and dances to young Indian boys and girls
- Instruments—drums, tambourines, wood blocks, cabasa
- Overhead projector

## Introduction

"**G**ood morning! From last class, what is another name for buffalo?" (bison) "And what did we read last time?" (a poem) "And what did we do with the poem to make it more expressive?" (We changed the way we read the poem.) "Yes. We changed the dynamic level; we read softly and loudly. We used inflection when asking questions. We discussed the feelings of the person in the poem. These feelings came across as we read it again."

## Process

"Let's return to your reading textbooks today. Please turn to page 481." Information in this passage describes what young boys and girls in Indian tribes were taught. Instruction included traditional myths, songs, and dances of their tribes. "I need a volunteer to read the first full paragraph on this page." Student reads the paragraph. "What two things, mentioned in the first sentence of the paragraph, remind us of how important music is in tribal life?" (songs and dances) "Good! You may put your textbooks away."

Display the transparency of Vocabulary Words and Questions. "Your reading teacher discussed these terms with you earlier. My definitions may not be exactly the same ones you've read, but let's review them and see if we learn anything new."

"May I have a student volunteer to read the definition for *civilization*?" Student reads the definition. Discuss terms within the definition that are unfamiliar to students. "What is meant by *arts*? Is music an art form?" (yes) "Is dance?" (yes) "Are painting and sculpting?" (yes) "Is theatre?" (yes) "Is literature?" (yes) "The abbreviation 'etc.' stands for the Latin term 'et cetera,' which means 'and so on.' "

"May I have another volunteer to read the definition for *culture*?" Student reads the definition. "Is music a part of one's culture?" (yes) "Choose a student to read aloud the first question beneath the vocabulary words and definitions. Student reads the question. "What are some instruments associated with Native American culture?" (drums and flute) Choose

> ### Vocabulary Words and Questions
> - Civilization—condition of people who have advanced far beyond a primitive level in government, arts, religion, science, etc.
> - Culture—knowledge, customs, and arts of a people or group at a certain time
> - What musical instruments have we heard that are associated with Native American culture?
> - What other art form is used with music to celebrate occasions such as hunts?
> - What are the Native American Indians' beliefs about the bear? What does the bear symbolize?
> - Could the bear be the subject of Native American legends and myths?

another student to read aloud the second question. Student reads the question. "What other art form is used with music to celebrate occasions such as hunts? We heard two pieces last week that had an art form included in their titles. Do you remember the buffalo and bear?" Choose another student to answer the question. (dances) "Good! Is dance an art form?" (yes) Choose another student to read the third question. Student reads the question. "What does the bear symbolize? What do Native Americans respect about the bear?" Choose another student to answer the question. (power, strength) "Yes! Last question." Choose a student to read the question. Student reads the question. "Could the bear be the subject of Native American myths and legends?" (yes) "I think so, too."

Display the transparency of "Tribal Chant."

Zu - ni, Ban - nock, Sioux, *(drums)*     *(tambourine)*     Ki - o - wa, Nav - a - jo, Chey-enne, too!

**Tribal Chant**

"Here are some rhythmic patterns using terms we have discussed in your reading selections. These patterns are based on what we have learned also in music class. I am going to read them aloud to you, and I would like you to repeat them back to me. Before we begin, look at the meter signature and tell me how many beats are in each measure." (four) "We have one measure here and one measure here." Point to each measure on the transparency.

"Please repeat after me." Read the first measure in rhythm. "Zuni, Bannock, Sioux," Students echo. "We have not talked about the Bannock tribe, but it is presented in your reading textbook." Repeat the first measure. Students echo. "In the second half of the first measure, the drums play sixteenth notes and the tambourine plays the quarter note." Point to the transparency. "The drum and tambourine are indicated here. Let's look at the next measure. I will read first." Read the measure according to the notated rhythmic pattern. "Kiowa, Navajo, Cheyenne, too." Students echo. Repeat this measure. Students echo. "Good. Let's take the pattern from the top. Remember, the pattern spoken in the first half of the first measure will be repeated on the drums and tambourine in the second half of the measure." Read the chant aloud with the class, modeling with hands the drum and tambourine parts at the appropriate times.

"The second time we read the entire chant, I would like the woodblocks to substitute for the drums and the cabasa to substitute for the tambourine." Demonstrate how to hold and play the cabasa. "Let me play the cabasa part while we perform the chant together." Provide preparatory count for simple quadruple meter. Perform the chant with the class, and play the cabasa at the appropriate time. "How many times will the cabasa be played?" (once) "Good. Let's get the instruments passed out!" Distribute the instruments to the class, having students assist with distribution. Explain to students that there are not enough instruments for everyone to play at one time. "Thank you for not playing the instruments and for waiting patiently. Those of you who do not have an instrument will receive and play one soon."

"Let's play the chant softly the first time. The letter 'p' in music is a symbol that comes from the Italian word *piano,* which means 'soft.' " Indicate the dynamic level by writing a "p" over the first measure on the transparency. "The second time we perform the chant, we will play loudly. The letter 'f' in music is a symbol that comes from the Italian word *forte,* which means 'loud.' " Indicate the dynamic level for the repeat by drawing a back slash to the right of the "p" and then writing an "f" beside the back slash.

"Raise your hand if you have a drum." Students respond. "Drummers, what is your rhythmic pattern?" (ti-di-ti-di) "Good. Let me hear you play it." Provide preparatory count for simple quadruple meter. Students play the pattern. "Excellent! Tambourines, where are you?" Students raise their hands. "What is your rhythmic pattern?" (ta) "Good. Let me hear you play it. I'll chant the drummer's syllables and you play on the quarter note. Ready?" Provide preparatory count for simple quadruple meter. "Excellent! I hope my instrumentalists on woodblocks and cabasa were listening! Woodblock players, is your rhythmic pattern like the drum pattern?" (yes) "Where is my cabasa player?" Student raises hand. "Do you play the same quarter note the second time through that the tambourines played the first time?" (yes)

"Everyone will chant the words both times. Who needs to be ready to play immediately after we say, 'Zuni, Bannock, Sioux'?" (drummers and tambourine players) "Great! Let's try the chant again and see how we do. Everyone ready?" Provide preparatory count for simple quadruple meter. Read the chant with the class and cue the instrumentalists. Cue the repeat. "Great job! Fantastic! Who has not played an instrument?" Students respond. "Would those of you nearest to classmates who have not played please give your instruments to them? If you have no one near you to receive an instrument, you get to play twice. Lucky you!"

"Let's remember the dynamic markings *p* and *f* this time. How will we speak and play the first time?" (softly) "The second time?" (loudly) "Good. Everyone ready?" Provide preparatory count for simple quadruple meter. Cue the instrumentalists. Cue the repeat. "Excellent job!"

## Summary

"Wow! Instruments add so much to our 'Tribal Chant,' don't they! You did a fantastic job of listening, looking, and playing. I hope that as you read more this week about Native American culture and think about past civilizations of people you study, you will see how important music was in their daily living, and in rituals and ceremonies. See you next time!"

# Lesson 6

## Focus
- Listening to Aaron Copland's *Lincoln Portrait*
- Writing creative descriptions based upon the listening selection
- Defining unfamiliar words in the text of the composition

## Related National Music Standards
- Grades K–4—Standards 6b, 6d, 8b
- Grades 5–8—Standards 8b

## Materials
- Recording of *Lincoln Portrait,* by Aaron Copland
- Transparency—study sheet for *Lincoln Portrait*
- Audio-playback equipment
- Overhead projector
- Notebook paper
- Pencils

## Introduction

Review the guided listening activity from Lesson 2. "Who remembers what composition we heard recently about a national park in Arizona?" ("Sunrise," from *Grand Canyon Suite*) "Do you remember that we did not know what the composition was about until after we shared our stories and poems?"

## Process

"Today we are going to hear another composition. You will hear an orchestra playing, but there are words in this composition, too. You will hear a narrator speaking. The narrator is going to give you hints about the composition's focus with the words he speaks. I have taken out the 'answer' so you won't hear the name of the person about whom this composition is written. You will not hear the narrator at the beginning. I would like you to listen to the music and create a story or an image you believe the music is suggesting. Listen for things like the tempo. What do we mean by 'tempo'?" (speed of the music) "Listen to the dynamic changes. What do they tell us?" (how loud or soft the music becomes) "Listen to the instruments that are used. Create your own little story. Write your description on your sheet of notebook paper."

Explain to students that they may write words, word lists, paragraphs, or even stories if they wish. The objective is to be creative while listening to the music. "I will stop the recording after the first two minutes and we will discuss what you have created!" Play the recording.

Share individual student responses with the class. Guide students to make associations between what they believe is happening and what elements of music help them develop their ideas. A king is walking in? Is he walking hurriedly? Majestically? Quietly?

"Let us continue and listen to the narration. The narrator will provide information that will help you identify the person. If you discover who the person is, please do not say your answer aloud. Some of you may need additional clues before you can respond. After listening, we will discuss also how the music alone helps you define the person. How does the music clarify the person for you? Do not let the narration do all of the work for you; listen to the music, too." Play the recording of *Lincoln Portrait* from the beginning of the narration to the end of the composition.

"Who thinks they know the person?" (Abraham Lincoln) "At what point in the narration did you realize that Abraham Lincoln was the person?" (excerpts from the Gettysburg Address; sixteenth president of the U.S.; stood six feet, four inches tall) "What other clues helped you? Did the narrator talk about slavery?" (yes) "Yes. The narrator used the word 'tyrannical.' Please turn your papers over."

"Your reading teacher has asked me to provide some vocabulary words this week." Display the transparency of the study sheet.

"Let's look at the vocabulary words at the bottom of this study sheet. I think these words are great for you to know because they were taken from the narration in the composition about Abraham Lincoln."

Define the words at the bottom of the study sheet with the class. Read to the class excerpts from the narrative that contain these words.

"This composition is entitled *Lincoln Portrait*. What about the music alone helped you form

## Study Sheet for *Lincoln Portrait* by Aaron Copland

Look at your description of the music you heard. What similarities, if any, do you find between your description and the impression Aaron Copland creates? List some on your sheet of paper.

Do you think the music portrays Abraham Lincoln? How?

Copland used Lincoln's words in this piece. Do you recognize any of them? From where do they come?

Do you think Copland chose particular quotations for specific places in the composition? Why? What changes occurred in the music when various excerpts of text were read?

Did you learn anything new about Abraham Lincoln from listening to Copland's music? If so, what?

*Vocabulary*
dogmas
disenthrall
bestride
tryrannical
melancholy
resolve

an image of Abraham Lincoln?" (big sound, sad at times, music sounded important, serious) "Did the composer use different combinations of sound?" (yes) "What instrument do you remember as having some solo passages?" (trumpet) "At the end of the piece, what instrument is heard in the background while the narrator reads about the honored dead?" (trumpet) "What piece have you heard played by the trumpet at military funerals or at the close of day?" ("Taps") "Did the composer create a melancholy feeling with the use of other instruments?" (yes) "With what instruments?" (woodwinds and strings) "Did he also create a solemn atmosphere with percussion and brass?" (yes)

## Summary

Review the purpose of the listening activity. "Today you heard a musical composition that included narration. You know that many authors, including Russell Freedman, have written books about Abraham Lincoln. Today you learned that an American composer, Aaron Copland, also wrote music about this president. Did you learn anything new about Abraham Lincoln from listening to the narration in Copland's piece? What about the music portrayed the composer?"

"Thanks for listening so well. If you would like me to read your stories or ideas you developed at the beginning of this activity, please put them on your desk and I will collect them. See you next time!"

# Lesson 7

## Focus
- Reading rhythmic patterns incorporating vocabulary words
- Identifying phrase structure within a composition

## Related National Music Standards
- Grades K-4—Standard 5a, 8b
- Grades 5-8—Standard 5a, 8b

## Materials
- Transparency—"Tipi Chant" (with each of the four sentences printed in a different color, including the fourth sentence in red)
- Visuals—strips with rhythmic patterns; three rhythmic patterns, written on the board
- *Invitations to Literacy: Level 5, Explore* (Boston: Houghton Mifflin, 1996); or teacher-generated list of words that fit the following visual strips: quarter note; two sixteenth notes and an eighth note; and four sixteenths and a quarter note
- Overhead projector
- Paper
- Pencils

## Introduction

"What did we listen to in our last class?" (a composition about Abraham Lincoln) "We learned that Aaron Copland was the composer of *Lincoln Portrait*, a musical composition that included Lincoln's own words. The man who served as narrator was James Earl Jones, and his voice is one that most of you might recognize as the voice of Darth Vader in the *Star Wars* movies and as Mufasa, in Walt Disney's *The Lion King*.

"Today we are going to begin the next unit in your reading textbook. Please get your textbook out and place it on your desk."

## Process

Display the transparency of "Tipi Chant."

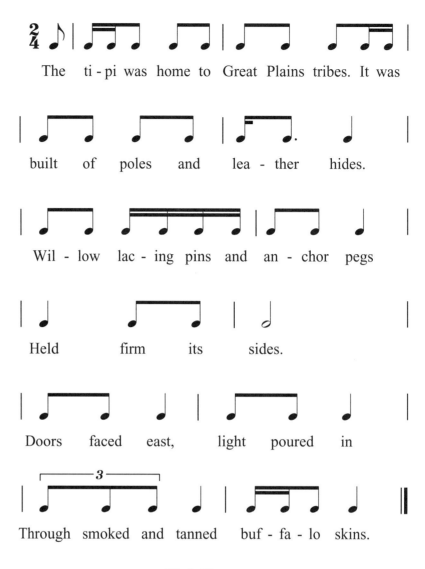

The ti-pi was home to Great Plains tribes. It was
built of poles and lea-ther hides.
Wil-low lac-ing pins and an-chor pegs
Held firm its sides.
Doors faced east, light poured in
Through smoked and tanned buf-fa-lo skins.

**Tipi Chant**

Direct students to look at the chant. "You will notice that I have printed the words of 'Tipi Chant' in color. I am not going to tell you why just yet. You will notice also that I have drawn lines beneath some words throughout the chant. These lines represent the beat. Join me in tapping the beat on your knees. Please tap quietly because what we are about to do requires a soft tapping of the beat in the background." Establish the beat for the class by tapping on an open palm and directing students to tap on their knees. "Say 'tap, tap, tap' on each pulse. I am going to let you continue tapping while I read the chant." Read words as students tap the beat.

"I created this chant using words in your textbook that described the tipi. I will read it again and ask that you tap once more, and then we will read it together." Read the chant. "Will you read it with me this time?" Provide preparatory count in simple duple meter. Read the chant in unison. "Good!"

"Let's go back and look at some words. What is a tipi?" (a home for some Native American tribes) "We are studying Native Americans from what specific location?" (the Great Plains) "Can anyone tell me what is meant by 'willow' in the phrase 'willow lacing pins'?" (made from the willow tree) "What are anchor pegs?" (wooden pegs used to hold the tipi in place)

"Keep the beat for me as I continue: 'Doors faced east, light poured in, Through smoked and tanned buffalo skins.' "

"Will you keep the beat and read this part with me?" Provide preparatory count for simple duple meter. Read aloud with the class. "Good!"

"Please look at the words in red, 'Doors faced east, light poured in.' " Display the first strip of rhythmic notation.

"What words do you find in red that will fit this pattern, 'ti–ti ta'?" (Doors faced east) "What other words?" (light poured in) "Good!"

Display the second strip of rhythmic notation.

"What words have we chanted in music class with this pattern?" (cho-co-late pie) "Good! What words in red fit this pattern?" (Through smoked and tanned)

Display the third strip of rhythmic notation.

"What words fit this rhythmic pattern?" (buffalo skins) "Good! Let's read the entire chant once together." Provide preparatory count for simple duple meter.

"Who can tell me how many phases are in the section that concludes with the words 'Held firm its sides'?" (three) "What on this chart tells you so?" (each phrase is written in a different color) "How could we determine these were phrases if we had no color to help us?" Guide students to each phase. "Examine the text to look for independent thoughts. How many complete sentences are there in the section ending with 'Held firm its sides'?" (three) "Are these sentences equal in length?" (no) "Just as sentences do not need to be the same length, musical phrases can be different lengths."

"How many phrases are there in the remainder of the chant, beginning with 'Doors faced east'?" (one)

"Please open your textbooks to page 492, 'Where Do They Live'? How did I come up with the words to our chant?" (using terms listed on pages 492 and 493) "As you look at these two pages, you can see how I composed our chant."

Display the visual strip with the following notation:

"In music class, with what syllable or with what word do we associate the quarter note?" (ta) "How many syllables are in 'ta'?" (one) Looking at page 492, what one-syllable words can you find that will match the quarter note?" (fuel, food, peg, gear, door, fur)

Display the visual strip with the following notation:

"What words on pages 462 and 463 fit this rhythmic pattern?" (lacing pins, buffalo, anchor pegs)

"I would like you to look at the three rhythmic patterns I have put on the board."

"The first pattern is composed of two eighth notes."

"Let's clap them together and say 'ti-ti' as we clap." Clap and say the pattern. "The second pattern is made up of four sixteenth notes."

"What words have we used in music class to remember the sound of four sixteenths?" (ti-di-ti-di or Reese's Pieces) "Let's clap and say this pattern." Clap and chant the pattern.

"The last pattern is made up of four sixteenth notes followed by one quarter note."

"Who would like to say this pattern?" (ti-di-ti-di ta or Reese's Pieces pie) "Let's clap and say this pattern together." Clap and chant the pattern.

"Look for words or groups of words on pages 462 and 463 in your textbook that will fit these three patterns. Write one example down for each pattern. How many examples should I find on your paper?" (three) "You may tap or chant each rhythmic pattern quietly to double-check your responses."

## Summary
"Today you looked carefully at phrases composed using words from your textbook. Do some of these words fit the rhythmic patterns we have studied in music class?" (yes) "How is a phrase in music like a complete sentence in reading?" (It expresses a thought.) "Remember to put your name on your papers and stack them in the center of your table. See you next time!"

# Lesson 8

## Focus
- Reading rhythmic patterns incorporating vocabulary words
- Performing word patterns organized in various meter signatures

## Related National Music Standards
- Grades K–4—Standards 5a, 8b
- Grades 5–8—Standards 5a, 8b

## Materials
- Transparencies—rhythmic patterns
- *Invitations to Literacy: Level 5, Explore* (Boston: Houghton Mifflin, 1996); or teacher-generated list of words that fit the following visual strips: quarter note; two sixteenth notes and an eighth note; and four sixteenths and a quarter note
- Overhead projector
- Paper
- Pencils

## Introduction

"Good morning! You need to clean your desks off except for your reading textbook, a pencil, and a piece of paper. Do you remember when I asked you to find terms in your reading text that would fit the pattern of four sixteenth notes, or 'ti-di-ti-di,' or 'Reese's Pieces'?" Today, let's look at some of the words you found in your textbook to match the rhythmic patterns I presented to you during the last lesson."

## Process

Display the transparency with the following notation:

"Let's review by clapping out some of your examples. Many of you listed 'sleeping pallets.' Let's clap our four sixteenth notes." Provide preparatory count for simple duple meter. Clap with the students. "Now let's say the words while clapping the pattern." Provide preparatory count for simple duple meter. Clap and say the pattern with the class. "Do the words 'sleeping pallets' fit?" (yes) "Good choice!"

Display the transparency with the following notation:

"Let's clap our two eighth-notes pattern." Provide preparatory count for simple duple meter. Clap with the students. "Good. Now read the words 'smoke flaps,' which I have written underneath the pattern, as you clap it once again." Provide preparatory count. Clap and chant with the class. "Do the words 'smoke flaps' fit this pattern?" (yes) "Good job!"

"How about the next pattern?" Display the transparency with the following notation.

"Let's clap this one." Provide preparatory count in simple duple meter. "Great! Now let's clap it together and say the words 'wooden anchor pegs,' which I have written beneath it." Provide preparatory count. Clap and chant with the class. "Do the words 'wooden anchor pegs' fit this pattern?" (yes) "Yes, they do. Good work!"

Display the transparency of the next pattern. "Let's try this one."

"What do we call this pattern in music class?" (triplet) "Yes! Remember we use 'cho-co-late' to help us perform this rhythmic pattern. Let's clap this pattern together." Provide preparatory count for compound duple meter. Clap the triplet with the class. "Good job. Let's clap this pattern and say together 'water bag.'" Provide preparatory count for compound duple meter. Clap and chant the pattern with the class. "Good job! Will 'anchor pegs' fit this pattern? Let's see." Provide preparatory count for compound duple meter. Clap and chant with the class. "Yes, it does! You did a great job matching reading vocabulary words with rhythmic patterns!"

Display the transparency with three rhythmic patterns (2/4, 3/4, and 4/4 meters). "Let's look at these patterns."

Point to the first rhythmic pattern. "How many beats are in each measure?" (two) "Yes. I'm going to establish the beat." Clap the beat for the class. "Clap the beat with me." Provide preparatory count for simple duple meter. Clap the beat with the class. "Good. Let's clap the pattern now." Provide preparatory count. Clap the pattern with the class. Under the first rhythmic pattern, write the sentence "Women put the tipis up." "Now let's say the sentence while we clap the pattern." Provide preparatory count. Clap and say the pattern with the class. " 'Women put the tipis up.' Now let's say the pattern and clap the beat, not the pattern." Provide preparatory count. Clap the beat and chant the pattern with the class. "Good job."

Point to the second rhythmic pattern. "Here is another pattern."

"What do you notice about this pattern?" (all the notes are quarter notes except the last one) "What kind of note is the last one?" (a dotted half note) "Yes. How many beats does a dotted half note get?" (three) "Yes. Let's clap this pattern together." Provide preparatory count for simple triple meter. Clap the pattern with the class. Under the second rhythmic pattern, write the sentence "Women erected the tipis they built." "Now let's clap and say the words beneath the pattern." Provide preparatory count. " 'Women erected the tipis they built.' Let's clap the beat and say the pattern. How many times will we clap in each measure?" (three) "On which beat or beats?" (first, second, and third) "Of the three beats in each measure, which is the most important?" (one) "Yes. One is the downbeat; it receives more weight. Let's say the pattern again and clap on the downbeats." Provide preparatory count. Clap the pattern with the class.

"Moving on!" Point to the third pattern.

"What's our meter signature?" (4/4) "Yes. I'm going to let you clap this one without me. What are you going to be tempted to do in the first measure?" (clap on two and four) "Yes. The half notes direct you not to. Try the whole pattern. Be careful in the third measure; it also contains a half note. The last measure contains what kind of a note?" (whole) "How many times will you clap in the last measure?" (once) "Good luck!" Provide preparatory count in simple quadruple meter. Count beats while students clap the pattern. "Let's try this again. Remember you will not clap on beats two and four in the first measure. Remember the last note receives four beats, but you clap only on which beat?" (one) Provide preparatory count. Count beats while students clap. "That was 95 percent! Good! Once more without a clap on beat two of the first measure. Make this your best effort!" Provide preparatory clap. Students clap the pattern. "Yes! Great job!"

Under the third rhythmic pattern, write the sentence "Sleeping pallets made of buffalo hides." "Let's add the words and make this exciting. Ready?" Provide preparatory count for simple quadruple meter. Students chant the words and clap the pattern. "Let's try this again. Remember our half-note friends. We are not giving them enough credit." Provide preparatory count.

"Much better. Let's try speaking and clapping the pattern again. Remember, 'sleep' gets two beats and 'ing' gets two beats. How many beats does the first syllable of 'buffalo' get?" (two) "Yes. How many beats does the word 'hides' get?" (four) "Yes. I would like 100 percent. I will say the beats aloud. You chant and clap. Hands up. Eyes up." Provide preparatory count. Speak the beats while class responds. "Yes. Improvement! Let's clap 'buffalo hides' once more." Provide preparatory count. Chant and clap with the class.

"Please take your pencil and write your name on your paper. After you have written your name, please write the number one. This is not a test!"

Display the transparency containing five rhythmic patterns.

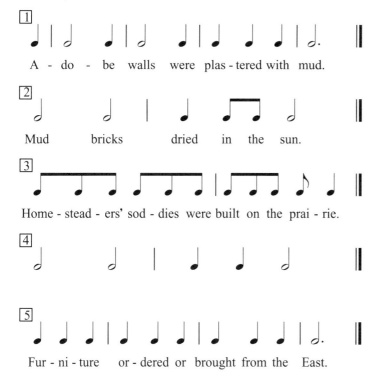

Point to the first rhythmic pattern. "Look at this pattern and decide whether the pattern is written in a meter of 2/4, 3/4, or 4/4. Write a 2 if you think this pattern is in 2/4 meter. Write a 3 if you think this pattern is in 3/4 meter, or write a 4 if you think this pattern is in 4/4 meter. You do not need to copy the pattern; just decide how many beats are in each measure of each pattern. I will speak the words written below the pattern. Listen to the pattern. 'Adobe walls were plastered with mud.' Speak the pattern again. Write your answer."

Point to the second rhythmic pattern. "Pattern number two: 'Mud bricks dried in the sun.'" Gesture the steady beat with your arm, as if bouncing a tennis ball on the downbeat and letting your arm rise on the upbeat. Repeat the pattern, saying the words and bouncing your arm. "Say it with me." Provide preparatory count in simple quadruple meter. " 'Mud bricks dried in the sun.' Again. One, two, ready, speak." Repeat with the class. "Is this pattern in 2/4, 3/4, or 4/4 meter? Don't tell me out loud; write your answer on your paper." Give students time to respond.

"We are going on. We are going where no man or woman has gone before! Point to the third rhythmic pattern. Look at this pattern with me. What are the primary types of notes we see in this pattern?" (eighth notes) "Our bottom number in the meter signature of this pattern will not be four; it probably will be what number?" (eight) "Yes. Now let's figure out what the top number will be if our bottom number is eight. We need to know how many eighth notes are in each measure. Count with me. One, two, three, four, five, six. How many eighth notes are in each measure?" (six) "Clap with me, please." Provide preparatory count in compound duple meter. Clap the pattern with the class.

"Now let's add the words." Provide preparatory count. " 'Homesteaders' soddies were built on the prairie.' Again." Provide preparatory count. Repeat the pattern with the class. "We are clapping six times in one measure. Can six divide into two?" (yes) "Let's put the emphasis, the weight, in two places. I'm going to clap the pattern and put a bit more weight on the first eighth note and the fourth eighth note. Listen." Provide preparatory count and emphasize the first and fourth pulses. "Clap and say the eighths with me, putting weight on the first and fourth eighth notes." Provide preparatory count. Clap and say the pattern with the class. "Good! This time, let's clap and say the words to the pattern, emphasizing the two beats that fall on the first and fourth eighth notes." Provide preparatory count. Clap and say the pattern with the class. "Good!"

"We have just a little time left. Please turn to page 497 in your reading textbook. Look with me on the bottom of the page. Do you see the words 'sod wall: two bricks thick'?" (yes) "Did I read that in rhythm?" (yes) "Yes, I did." Write the fourth rhythmic pattern on the transparency.

"Please copy this fourth rhythmic pattern onto your paper." Point to the fourth pattern on the transparency. "Under this pattern, what will you write?" (sod wall:

two bricks thick) "Make sure your words are written beneath the appropriate notes. Space your words so that they fit where they need to. Also, put the correct meter signature at the beginning of the pattern. Do you see any measure containing six eighth notes?" (no) "Do you see any measure that has a value equaling six eighth notes?" (no) "So what meter signature will we not consider correct for this pattern?" (6/8) "Right. What are our choices then?" (2/4, 3/4 or 4/4). "Choose one of these meter signatures for your answer. You may close your textbook and put your paper face down in the center of your table."

## Summary

Point to the fifth rhythmic pattern. "Someone raise a hand and tell me what meter signature this pattern is in. 'Furniture ordered or brought from the East.'" Choose a student to answer. (3/4) "Good! Are the papers in? Thanks for listening so closely today. Your word choices for the rhythmic assignment were very good! Great job matching vocabulary words with rhythmic patterns! See you next time!"

# Lesson 9

## Focus
- Singing a parody song
- Describing "tall tales"

## Related National Music Standards
- Grades K–4—Standards 1b, 2b
- Grades 5–8—Standard 1c

## Materials
- Poster with definition of tall tale (see Introduction)
- Transparencies—"Down in the Valley"; and "Pecos Bill"
- Overhead projector
- Instruments—drums, tambourines

### Introduction
"Good morning! Who can tell me what a tall tale is?" (a story that is exaggerated; a story that stretches the truth) "Let's look at Webster's definition of a tall tale." Display the poster. " 'A narrative of some event or sequence of actual, legendary, or fictitious events,'—What do you think 'fictitious' means? (fictional; make-believe)—'usually imaginatively composed with the intent to amuse.' Will tall tales be comical or will they be tragic?" (comical) "Yes. Now you have two definitions of tall tale, and they are similar, aren't they?" (yes)

### Process
"How many of you know the song 'Down in the Valley'?" Display the transparency and sing the song for the class.

### Down in the Valley
Down in the valley, valley so low,
Hang your head over; hear the wind blow.
Hear the wind blow, dear; hear the wind blow.
Hang your head over; hear the wind blow.
—*Kentucky folk song*

"I will sing it again, but I'd like you to turn your chairs so that you face me."

"Use your hands to tap the steady beat as I sing this song again. I'll get you started. Knees, first, then hands." Model for the class. " 'Knees hands hands, knees hands hands.' Try it with me." Provide preparatory count in simple triple meter. Pat and clap with the class. Sing the song while the class continues to keep time. "Who can tell me what meter we are in?" (three) "Which beat was the heaviest?" (one) "Which beat is the downbeat?" (the first beat) "Yes. Remember the arm movements we practiced last time to show the downbeat and rebound? Let's practice those movements now." Provide preparatory count. " 'Down lift up, down lift up, down lift up, ready and stop.' Good."

Display the transparency with "Pecos Bill." "Take a look at my new song!"

"You will recognize many words in this song. They all describe a tall tale character you will be reading about this week. What is his name?" (Pecos Bill) "Right! And I am singing my song to the tune of 'Down in the Valley'!" Read each line and have the class repeat it. Guide students to use inflection. "I'd like your mountaintop to be quite high in pitch and quite intense in volume. Will you say 'from a mountaintop' as if you are speaking from a big, white, majestic mountaintop? With gusto, let me hear you!" Students respond.

"Great. Can we read these words using the rhythm of the melody in 'Down in the Valley'? Let's try it and see. First, let's get the beat going. I'll bring you in." Provide preparatory count in simple triple meter. Read the words and pat the beat with the class. "Good!"

> ## Pecos Bill
> ### Sung to the tune of "Down in the Valley"
> Howled with the coyotes,
> Outran most deer,
> Rode a wild cougar,
> Lassoed a steer (*spoken:* from a MOUNTAIN TOP!)
>
> Harnessed a twister,
> (*spoken:* A real buckaroo!)
> Made many landmarks,
> Loved Slue-Foot Sue.
>
> We've reached the end of
> Our tale of the West!
> Of all the great cowboys,
> Bill is the best!

Choose students to maintain the downbeat on drums. "[Name of a student], will you tap your drum on the downbeat of each measure? What beat will you tap, the first, second, or third?" (first) "We'll think of your drum as Bill's boot hitting the ground with each step he makes." Choose other students to play the second and third beats of each measure using the tambourines. "[Name of a student], you will play the tambourine on the second and third beats of the measure. Bill doesn't look where he's going sometimes, and every once in a while he gets cacti stuck in the spurs of his boots. He shakes his boots a couple of times with each step, hoping that the cacti will break loose. We'll hear the spurs jingle when you shake your tambourine!"

"Let's listen to the drum and tambourine accompaniment alone before we sing the song. I'll set the tempo and count the beats for you." Provide preparatory count in simple triple meter. Count the beats while students play instruments. "Good! Remember not to rush the tempo. You are setting the tempo for us before we sing. Now let's join them and sing the words to 'Pecos Bill.'

Instrumentalists, will you play a two-measure introduction for us?" Provide preparatory count for the instrumentalists. Cue the instrumentalists. Hum the starting pitch during the introduction. Sing the song with the class. Guide instrumentalists by imitating their movements on respective instruments.

## Summary

"Great job! I hope that you will enjoy reading about Pecos Bill this week! What are some words in my song that are similar to words your reading teacher discussed this morning? What words in my song mean the same thing as 'cowpoke'?" (cowboy; buckaroo) "Was Pecos Bill a buckaroo"? (yes) "Was Pecos Bill a cowboy?" (yes) "What does 'harnessed a twister' mean?" (he lassoed a tornado) "Yes. 'Lasso' is one of your vocabulary words. Does anyone know how the Great Salt Lake was formed, according to the legend of Pecos Bill?" Wait for students to respond. "His hold on the twister was so tight, that the twister broke down and cried. The tears from the twister filled up the hole that we know today as the Great Salt Lake! How's that for a tall tale!"

"I brought my copy of *Pecos Bill* to share with you this week. Robin Williams is narrating the story on cassette tape. Perhaps your reading teacher will allow you to listen to the recording sometime before I see you next time for our hootenanny! Have a good day!"

# Lesson 10

## Focus
- Singing appropriate melodies for a hootenanny
- Identifying and defining vocabulary words in the melodies
- Identifying the verse and refrain in musical form

## Related National Music Standards
- Grades K–4—Standards 1b, 6a
- Grades 5–8—Standard 1c

## Materials
- Transparencies—"Yellow Rose of Texas," "Deep in the Heart of Texas," "Home on the Range" (see music textbooks listed below); and "My Home's in Montana," in *The Music Connection*, Grade 5 (Parsippany, NJ: Silver Burdett Ginn, 1995)
- Recording of "Yellow Rose of Texas," in *The Music Connection*, Grade 4; or *Share the Music*, Grade 5 (New York: Macmillan/McGraw-Hill, 1995, 2000)
- Recording of "Deep in the Heart of Texas," *The Music Connection*, Grade 3; or *World of Music*, Grade 6 (Parsippany, NJ: Silver Burdett Ginn, 1988, 1991)
- Recording of "Home on the Range," in *World of Music*, Grade 6; or *The Music Connection*, Grade 5
- "Home on the Range," in *Invitations to Literacy: Level 5, Explore* (Boston: Houghton Mifflin, 1996); *World of Music*, Grade 6; or *The Music Connection*, Grade 5
- Audio-playback equipment
- Overhead projector
- Hootenanny-style dress (optional)—denim skirt, shirt, bandanna, boots, and hat

## Introduction

"Good morning! Who remembers what is another name for lasso?" (lariat) "Good. What's another name for cowpoke?" (Cowboy, buckaroo) "Great! What was the name of the buckaroo we sang about last time?" (Pecos Bill) "Yes! Who can tell me something about Pecos Bill?" (He invented the lasso. He taught others how to drive cattle.) "What else did he do?" (He rode a tornado.) "According to the legend, how was the Great Salt Lake created?" (The tornado cried and its tears formed the lake.) "What river is named for him?" (the Pecos) "This river flows into the Rio Grande River. What state is bordered on its west side by the Rio Grande?" (Texas)

## Process

"We are going to sing some songs this morning about Pecos Bill's favorite state. Have any of you ever lived in Texas? Visited Texas? Wanted to go to Texas?" Students respond.

"Our first song is called 'The Yellow Rose of Texas.' " Display the transparency with the lyrics to "Yellow Rose of Texas." "I am going to read the words aloud. Read silently along with me; I may pause every so often and let you fill in a word or two." Read the lyrics to the class and provide opportunities for them to say the words aloud to the first verse.

"Are we talking about a flower in this song or a girl?" (a girl) "Yes. We are going to find out more about this girl in the refrain. Who can tell me what a refrain is?" (the part of the song that is repeated) "Yes. Let's look at the refrain." Read aloud the lyrics to the refrain, allowing students to fill in the words. "Let's listen to the first verse and refrain on the recording, and then sing the refrain after the second verse is sung." Play the recording. Direct the students' attention to the refrain on the transparency as it is played on the recording. Cue the students and sing with them on the second refrain. "Let's sing the entire song and clap the beat when we sing the refrain each time." Play the recording again and clap with the students on the refrain.

"Here's another song about Texas." Display the transparency with the lyrics to "Deep in the Heart of Texas." "Let's read the lyrics to 'Deep in the Heart of Texas.' " Read the lyrics aloud in rhythm, clapping the eighth-note pattern before the words "deep in the heart of Texas." "How many of you know this song or recognize it by the rhythm of the lyrics?" Students respond. "Let's sing it together. Here we go!" Play the recording and sing with the class, clapping eighth-note patterns. "Everyone say, 'Yee-haw!' " Students respond.

"Our next song, 'Home on the Range,' is in your reading textbook. Please turn in your textbooks to page 511. Look at the lyrics of the song as I play it. Listen carefully to the words on the recording and compare them with the words in your textbook. Let's see if we find differences. Are we ready? Everyone say, 'Yee-haw!' " Students respond. Play the recording. Listen with the class. Display the transparency with the lyrics to "Home on the Range." "Now let's sing the song using the words on the transparency; they match the words on the recording." Play the recording. Sing the song with the class. "Great! Wonderful job!" Pat the beat of the last few measures of the accompaniment. "In what meter is the song, two or three?" (three) "Good!"

" 'My home's in Montana, I wear a _____.' " Pull your bandanna to provide the answer. (bandanna) "Yes! Does anyone know this song?" Students respond. Display the transparency with the lyrics to "My Home's in Montana." Read the lyrics aloud to the class, providing opportunities for them to fill in missing words. " 'With my foot in the stirrup, I gallop for aye.' What does the word 'aye' mean?" Choose a student to be the "Dictionary Person." "Please get a dictionary from the bookcase and look up the word 'aye.' " Student responds. "Thank you. I'll get back to you in a minute! Let's listen to the soloist on the recording during the first verse, and then let's sing the second and third verses." Play the recording. Point to the lyrics on the transparency. "You are singing words to the second and third verses." Cue the students to sing. Pat the beats again at the ending. "In what meter is this song?" (three) "Good! Ask the student with the dictionary to read the definitions of "aye." Assist the student if necessary. "Which definition of 'aye' should we choose, according to the way it is used in the phrase 'I gallop for aye?' " (forever; always). "Yes! Yee-haw!" Students respond.

## Summary

"Good job today! Great singing! Did we hear songs with two-part form?" (yes) "Did we hear songs with a meter of two and songs with a meter of three?" (yes)

"Great listening! See you next time!"

# Lesson 11

## Focus
- Defining vocabulary words associated with specific types of musical compositions
- Listening to specific types of musical compositions

## Related National Music Standards
- Grades K–4—Standards 6a, 6b, 6d, 8b
- Grades 5–8—Standard 6a, 8b

## Materials
- Recording of "Fantasie-Impromptu in C# minor," op. 66, by Frederic Chopin
- Recording of "Fantasy on a Theme by Thomas Tallis," by Ralph Vaughan Williams
- Transparency—definitions of *fantasy, fantasia* and *impromptu*
- Audio-playback equipment
- Overhead projector

## Introduction

"**G**ood morning! This week you will be learning more about the kinds of stories you are reading. Your reading teacher will be discussing the terms *fantasy* and *realism* with you. Is the story of Pecos Bill a true story?" (no) "What term do we use to describe the kind of story 'Pecos Bill' is?" (a tall tale) "Yes. You remember that tall tales are based on fictitious characters. I understand that you have discussed another term this week that has to do with tall tales, with writing that is greatly exaggerated. This word begins with an 'h.' Who can tell me what word I'm looking for?" (hyperbole) "Good!"

## Definitions

*fantasy*—poem, play, or story showing much imagination or having fanciful ideas: "Peter Pan" is a fantasy.

*fantasia*—musical composition written according to no fixed or set form; medley of various tunes or themes.

*impromptu*—(adjective) without preparation; offhand; an impromptu picnic; (noun) something done or performed without preparation.

## Process

"Let's look at definitions on the transparency." Display the transparency.

"These definitions do not come from your book, but from dictionaries I have consulted. The first one is the definition for 'fantasy.' Would someone like to read this definition aloud?" Call on a student volunteer. "Thank you." Student reads definition aloud. "A poem, play, or story—would a tall tale fit within this description?" (yes) "Good!"

"Our next word is 'fantasia.' Who would like to read the definition for fantasia?" Call on a student volunteer. "Thank you." Student reads the definition aloud. "Good!" Repeat the definition to the class. "If a fantasia is not based upon a set form, would we be able to identify its parts, or label its parts with letters?" (no) Student asks whether Walt Disney's film *Fantasia* could be an example. "Yes! Are you familiar with that movie?" (yes) "Are there many pieces of music put together in that film?" (yes) "And what word in the definition of 'fantasia' means a collection of musical pieces?" (medley) "Yes! I am glad you thought of that film!"

"Who would like to read the definition for 'impromptu'?" Call on a student volunteer. "Thank you. Everyone follow along." Student reads the definition aloud. "Good! An impromptu picnic: that's the kind of picnic that you would have if you came home one afternoon and Mom or Dad said, 'We're going on a picnic. Put your things down and hurry to the car.' However, if they have an agenda or schedule—at 3:00, this is planned; at 3:30, something else will take place; at 4:00, still something else is planned—then is that afternoon's picnic impromptu?" (no) "No. The schedule is set. They have prepared it ahead of time."

"How many of you like to do things impromptu? Spur of the moment? Spontaneously? Without much planning?" Students respond. "Have many of you like to plan ahead? You want to know what's ahead of you?" Students respond. "A few of us do!"

"Many people give impromptu performances each day. Some examples might include a student who can recite a poem instantly without having to look over it ahead of time; a basketball player who sinks three pointers without practicing; a musician who makes up his or her composition as he or she plays it; an actor who makes up lines, who 'ad libs' to cover a memory lapse, to create interest, or just to fill time."

"We are going to listen to two pieces of music this morning. One is called a 'Fantasie-Impromptu.' The composer of this piece, Frederic Chopin, created something for the piano that is both an impromptu and a fantasy." Play the recording of "Fantasie-Impromptu." "Did you hear the tempo change?" (yes) "Did you feel a change of mood at tempo changes?" (yes) "Does the ending sound like the beginning?" (yes) "Why?" (has the same melody, fast tempo)

"Let's listen to another piece. This one is called 'Fantasia on a Theme by Thomas Tallis' and is by Ralph Vaughan Williams. Thomas Tallis was the composer of the theme that Ralph Vaughan Williams used as the basis for his composition. You have written about a theme in this class. Your theme is not musical, but the idea is much the same. Your teacher may assign the topic, or theme; 'flowers,' for example.

Will everyone in this room write the exact same paragraph about flowers?" (no) "In music, many melodies have been used as themes for musical compositions."

"The fanatasia we are going to hear features a family of instruments that we have heard in music class. After we listen, I am going to ask four students to name one instrument that belongs to this particular family." Play the first minute of "Fantasy on a Theme by Thomas Tallis." "Who can tell me what family of instruments they heard?" (the strings) "Yes! Who can give me the name of one instrument in the string family?" (violin) "Good! Who can give me another?" (double bass) "Another?" (cello) "Yes! One more." (viola) "Good for you! Let's say the names of the stringed instruments, from the smallest to the largest." (violin, viola, cello, double bass) "Of the violin and viola, which has the higher range?" (violin) "Good for you! If I am a member of a string quartet, how many others play with me?" (three) "Great!"

## Summary
"We now know that the term fantasy has many meanings. In reading, we know it means what?" (a make-believe story) "Yes. In music, it also may be called a fantasia. What is a fantasia?" (a musical form with no set form or a medley of various tunes) "Good job today. See you next time!"

# Lesson 12

**Focus**
- Listening to and singing a ballad

**Related National Music Standards**
- Grades K–4—Standards 1b, 6b
- Grades 5–8—Standards 1c

**Materials**
- Transparency—"John Henry" (see music textbooks listed below)
- Recording of "John Henry," *The Music Connection,* Grade 5 (Parsippany, NJ: Silver Burdett Ginn, 1995); or *World of Music,* Grade 5 (Parsippany, NJ: Silver Burdett Ginn, 1988, 1991)
- Audio-playback equipment
- Overhead projector

## Introduction

"Good morning! What is a *legend*? You have seen that word before in your reading." (a tale, a myth) "Can a legend be based on fact?" (yes) "Can a legend center on a real person?" (yes) "What happens to the truth when you go from a legend to a tall tale?" (The truth is stretched; it is exaggerated.) "Good! What was the other term we used last time to describe exaggerated truth?" (hyperbole)

## Process

"One legendary person your reading teacher discussed with you is someone I remember learning about when I was in elementary school. Who can tell me what legendary figure you have talked about recently?" (John Henry) "Yes. Why is John Henry remembered?" (He competed against a machine and he won.) "What kind of machine did he compete against?" (a steam drill) "What tool did John Henry use?" (a hammer) "Yes! He had a hammer in each hand."

Display the transparency with the lyrics to "John Henry." "Let's look at the words as we listen to this song about John Henry. If you know this song, will you pretend for a minute or two that you have never heard it before and just listen?" Play the recording.

"What happened to John Henry?" Call on a student. (He died because he worked so hard that his heart broke.) "Yes. Let's examine this song from a musical standpoint. Who can tell me how many phrases are in each verse?" Call on a student. (five) "Yes! Who knows what phrase is repeated in each verse?" (the fourth) "Great job!"

"Who can tell me what the meter signature is in this song?" Call on a student. (4/4) "If we look at this song, note by note, of what value are most of the notes we see?" (eighth notes) "Wonderful! Excellent job! The one hundred thousand dollar question! You know I don't have one hundred thousand dollars to give away, but I'll ask it anyway! For one hundred thousand imaginary dollars, was the soloist singing with accompaniment or without?" (pause) "Did you hear instruments playing while he was singing or did you hear him by himself?" (by himself) "Congratulations!" Give student imaginary prize money.

"I'd like you to join the gentleman singing on the recording. Sing with as much energy and enthusiasm as he does! Let's also snap on the upbeats. Watch me at the beginning. I'm snapping on beats two and four. Here we go!" Play the recording. Sing with the class and snap on beats two and four. "What instrument played the ending?" (harmonica) "Very good."

"Fill in the imaginary blank. I'm looking for a word that I have never discussed with you. I have heard your reading teacher say it. This word is a musical term. Here is the clue. Legends in literature are often the subjects of 'blank' in music. I'll say it again." Repeat the clue. "What is the musical term for a song that tells a story?" (folk song) "Very good! Your answer is very close, but I'm looking for a word that begins with the letter 'b.' " The 'blank' of John Henry, the 'blank' of Pecos Bill, the 'blank' of Casey Jones? B-a-l-l-a-d. Ballad!"

## Summary
"What is a ballad?" (a song that tells a story) "Is 'John Henry' a ballad?" (Yes) "When your reading teacher refers to tall tales, legends, and stories this week, I want you to remember this word. When she discusses the story of John Henry, I want you to tell her that you sang the (ballad) of John Henry. Have a good week! See you next time!"

# Lesson 13

## Focus
- Singing a ballad
- Creating a sentence using words that describe the ballad

## Related National Music Standards
- Grades K–4—Standard 1b
- Grades 5–8—Standard 1c

## Materials
- Transparency—"John Henry" (see music textbooks listed below)
- Recording of "John Henry," in *The Music Connection*, Grade 5 (Parsippany, NJ: Silver Burdett Ginn, 1995); or *World of Music*, Grade 5 (Parsippany, NJ: Silver Burdett Ginn, 1988, 1991)
- *John Henry,* by Julius Lester (New York: Dial Books, 1994)
- *Peter and the Wolf,* by Erna Voight, adapted from Prokofiev (Boston: David R. Godine, 1980)
- Audio-playback equipment
- Overhead projector

## Introduction
"**G**ood morning! What was the name of the song we learned in our last class?" ("John Henry") "Yes! Three of you have reminded me this morning to ask you about the word I wanted you to remember regarding what type of song we sang last time?" (ballad) "Yes. Spell it, everyone." Spell the word with the class. "Good. What is a ballad?" (a song that tells a story) "Great!"

## Process
"Guess what your media specialist brought to me today?" Display the book *John Henry.* "Here is a book about John Henry. This book is illustrated by Jerry Pickney. Mr. Pickney is a wonderful illustrator. Your media specialist also asked me to ask you to whom the Caldecott Award is awarded each year." (an illustrator) "This book received the Caldecott Award! I hope that you will check out this book and look carefully at the illustrations. They are beautiful!"

"We are going to sing 'John Henry' again this morning, since your reading teacher would like to hear it." Display the transparency with the lyrics to "John Henry."

"Who remembers how many people were singing this song on the recording?" (one) "Was a man singing or a woman?" (man) "Good. Did he sing with or without accompaniment?" (without) "Yes. He sang the melody by himself."

"Here we go!" Sing the song with the class. "Good job! Who remembers what instrument we heard at the very end of the song?" (harmonica) "Yes! And how many phrases are in each verse?" (five) "Yes! The word 'phrase' is one of your spelling words this week. Could you create a sentence using this word from the information you just gave me?" (There are five phrases in each verse of "John Henry.") "Great! What is our music definition of the word 'phrase'?" (A phrase is a musical sentence.)

"Let me share with you what we will be doing next time. You are learning about an animal in your reading selection this week. That animal is a _____?" (wolf) "Yes. How many of you are familiar with the musical story of 'Peter and the Wolf'?" Students raise hands. "Good! Who can tell me something about this musical story? Is this story written for one musical instrument?" (no) "Two instruments?" (no) "What is so interesting about the way this story is told? What is so interesting about the characters in this musical setting?" (The instruments represent characters in the story.) "Yes!"

"Does anyone remember what happens to the duck in this story?" (He is eaten by the wolf.) "How do you know that the duck is swallowed whole?" (You can hear the instrument still playing softly. The duck is inside the wolf's stomach.) "Good!"

Display the book *Peter and the Wolf*, by Erna Voight. "What do you notice about this book?" (It has music written on the pages.) "Yes! And beside the music what do you see?" (an instrument) "Yes. Each theme and instrument you see in this book and hear in the recording represents a character in the story. This book really helps you identify the sound with the character, doesn't it? Next time, we will begin listening to *Peter and the Wolf*. The music you will hear is written by a Russian composer by the name of Sergei Prokofiev. I will also bring the book to class and some posters of the instruments you will hear in the music."

## Summary

"Good singing today! Before we put 'John Henry' aside, who can tell me in what meter this ballad is written?" (4/4) "Is the rhythm of this melody lively or calm?" (lively)

"Good! We've been learning about note values in music class. Who can tell me what note value is used the most in this ballad?" (the eighth note) "Good! Yes. In fact, all the notes in the first phrase are eighth notes except which one?" (the last one) "Yes!"

"Great job! See you next time."

# Lesson 14

## Focus
- Listening to *Peter and the Wolf*
- Identifying musical themes in the composition
- Discussing musical themes as characters in the story

## Related National Music Standards
- Grades K–4—Standards 6b, 6d
- Grades 5–8—Standard 6a

## Materials
- Recording of *Peter and the Wolf*, by Prokofiev
- *Peter and the Wolf*, by Erna Voight, adapted from Prokofiev (Boston: David R. Godine, 1980)
- Posters of instruments (Bowmar Series, for example)
- Drawings of characters (from Voight book, children's books, or recording covers)
- Audio-playback equipment

## Introduction

"Who remembers the name of the musical composition we are going to listen to today?" (*Peter and the Wolf*) "Yes. Please raise your hand if you have heard this piece before." Students respond. "Good. If you have not heard this piece before, today is your lucky day!"

## Process

Display book and leaf through pages for class. "Why do you think I like this book?" Call on a student. (It has pictures.) "Yes. What else do you see?" (musical instruments and lines of music) "Yes! The themes are written out beside the instruments that play them. Will an instrument represent each character in the story?" (yes) "Yes. We need to listen carefully when the narrator introduces the characters so that we can identify a particular instrument and theme with each character in the story."

Display posters of instruments. "As you listen to this story, remember that the posters of instruments displayed at the front of the room are the instruments you will hear in the recording. The instruments on the posters are the violin, flute, oboe, clarinet, bassoon, horn, and tympani."

Play the recording. Point to each poster as the narrator introduces the characters. Point to the tympani as "guns" are introduced.

["Early one morning ... "] Display the drawing of Peter. Place the drawing beside the poster of the violin.

["On the branch of a big tree ... "]) Display the drawing of a bird. Place the drawing beside the poster of the flute.

["Just then a duck came waddling ...") Display the drawing of a duck. Place the drawing beside the poster of the oboe.

Point to the poster of the flute when that instrument sounds with the oboe. Point to the drawings of the duck and the bird to indicate the pair conversing in the story.

["Suddenly something caught Peter's attention."] Display the drawing of a cat. Place the drawing beside the poster of the clarinet.]

["Grandfather came out ... ") Display the drawing of Grandfather. Place the drawing beside the poster of the bassoon. Write the word "bassoon" on the board.

Point to the posters of the bassoon and the violin as the narrator tells of Grandfather taking Peter back home.

["No sooner had Peter gone, than out of the forest ... "] Display the drawing of a wolf. Place the drawing beside the poster of the horn.

Show the class Erna Voight's illustration of Peter catching the wolf by the tail.

["Peter tied the other end of the rope to the tree."] Stop the recording.

## Summary
"Is Peter represented only by the violin or do we hear the violin playing a melody with orchestral accompaniment?" (a melody with accompaniment) "Good! Do you think the bassoon sounds like a grandfather?" (yes) "Why?" (It plays slowly and it sounds very deep and quite old.) "Good listening! Who heard more than one horn playing the part of the wolf?" Students raise hands. "You are right. We will listen to the conclusion of *Peter and the Wolf* next week. Thank you for listening carefully and for sitting attentively!"

# Lesson 15

## Focus
- Listening to *Peter and the Wolf*
- Identifying musical themes in the composition
- Discussing musical themes as characters in the story

## Related National Music Standards
- Grades K–4—Standards 6b, 6d
- Grades 5–8—Standard 6a

## Materials
- Recording of *Peter and the Wolf*, by Prokofiev
- *Peter and the Wolf*, by Erna Voight, adapted from Prokofiev (Boston: David R. Godine, 1980)
- Posters of instruments (Bowmar Series, for example)
- Drawings of characters (from Voight book, children's books, or recording covers)
- Audio-playback equipment

## Introduction
Display posters and drawings at the front of the room.

"Good morning! Who remembers where we left off in the story of *Peter and the Wolf?*" (Peter had lassoed the wolf.) "Yes! Who helped Peter catch the wolf?" (the bird) "Good! What did the bird do to help?" (He distracted the wolf by flying around his face.) "Yes! Where did one end of the lasso end up?" (around the wolf's tail) "And the other end?" (around a tree) "Great job remembering! What happened to the duck?" (He was swallowed whole by the wolf.)

"Who can tell me which instrument represents Peter?" (the violin) "Good! What about the bird?" (the flute) "Yes, and the duck?" (oboe) "Good! The cat?" (the clarinet) "The grandfather?" (the bassoon) "The wolf?" (horn) "What instrument represents the hunters, although we have not heard their entrance as of yet?" (tympani) "Great!"

## Process
"I am going to play the capture of the wolf again to prepare us for the conclusion." Play the recording. ["And now, this is how things stood ... "] Pause

recording after hunters enter and begin walking toward Peter and the others. "Who can determine the direction the hunters are taking by listening to their theme and the drums?" (They are walking toward Peter and the wolf because the marching and drums are louder.)

["And now … now imagine the triumphant procession."] Pause recording after Peter's theme is played. "How is this theme different from the first time we heard Peter?" (This is bigger, slower, more majestic; important.) Continue playing recording. Pause after all instruments are playing. "As we listen to the other instruments and imagine the procession, do you think the characters are dancing, jumping up and down, or marching?" (marching) "Why?" (The beat is slow, steady and very heavy.) "Good for you! Remember, this is a triumphant procession; one that is majestic, dignified, impressive to watch. If we imagine them marching, in what meter do you suppose the music is written?" (two) "Yes!"

["And if you listen very carefully, you can hear the duck … "] Pause recording after oboe is heard. "Does the oboe theme sound as merry as it did at the story's beginning?" (no) Play the recording to the end.

## Summary

"Good listening today! Some of you have shared with me different endings to this story. In the musical story we just heard, do we learn anything more about the characters other than the fact that they were taking the wolf and the duck quacking inside him to the zoo?" (no) "You can compare this story's ending with another version of *Peter and the Wolf*. Your reading teacher has a video of this story that you will watch later this week. It may present an ending different from the one we just heard!"

"Watch closely, and next time, we'll discuss what you saw in the video. Have a good day!"

# Lesson 16

## Focus
- Performing rhythmic patterns based upon familiar text with instrumental accompaniment
- Identifying propaganda within the text of a composition

## Related National Music Standards
- Grades K–4—Standards 5a, 2b
- Grades 5–8—Standard 5a

## Materials
- Transparency—rhythmic "Propaganda Patterns" (with accent marks in red on each beat)
- Classroom instruments—tambourines, drums, woodblocks, guiro, claves, maracas, cabasa, cymbals, castanets
- Overhead projector

## Introduction

"Good morning! I understand that you are learning about propaganda in your reading this week. What is 'propaganda'?" (information that is presented to persuade) "Yes! That's a good answer. Propaganda is used to promote or discourage a cause or group."

## Process

"You have been studying tales and legends of the wolf this week. You also have examined propaganda about the wolf. I have taken some of the information that has been presented to you and have used it to create a parody song that we will learn next time. Today, we are going to look at some phrases that we will perform with classroom instruments. These are familiar phrases, and you have probably heard them before. I think that they are somewhat propagandistic because they were created to raise our fears."

Display the transparency. "Let's read the first example aloud." Provide preparatory count in compound duple meter. Read with class.

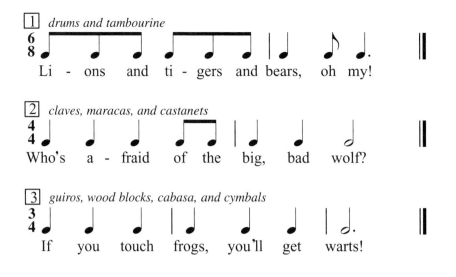

1 *drums and tambourine*

Li - ons and ti - gers and bears, oh my!

2 *claves, maracas, and castanets*

Who's a - fraid of the big, bad wolf?

3 *guiros, wood blocks, cabasa, and cymbals*

If you touch frogs, you'll get warts!

## Propaganda Patterns

"What did we accent as we read this example?" (the main beat) "Good. Let's look at the next example."

Display second example on the transparency. "Let's read this one aloud." Provide preparatory count in simple duple meter. Speak the pattern with the class.

Sing the question for the class. "Who recognizes this question?" (The three little pigs sang this question.) "Yes!"

Display the third example. "I made this one up for you. The idea for this sentence comes straight out of your reading textbook!" Read the sentence aloud for the class.

"Read this sentence with me this time." Provide preparatory count in simple triple meter. Read aloud with the class.

"Good! Let's read it again, and this time we'll tap two fingers on an open palm whenever we see the red accent mark I have drawn to represent the beat. Are we tapping the rhythm of the words or the steady beat?" (the steady beat) "Yes!"

"Hands ready?" Provide preparatory count for simple triple meter. Read and tap with the class. "Great! Can you tap the beat with me as we read the second example?" Provide preparatory count for simple quadruple meter. Read and tap the second example. "Good! And now, the first example."

Provide preparatory count for compound duple meter. Read and tap the first example. "Great job!"

"We will be using instruments this morning. The beats you have just tapped will be played on instruments." Choose students to assist with distribution of instruments. "Thank you for keeping your instruments at rest while the others wait to receive theirs! I'm looking to see who is responsible and ready to continue." Assist students if necessary. "Who does not have an instrument?" Check to see that all students have an instrument.

Call on students with claves to hold them up. "Remember, when you hold the claves, you need to make a fist with one hand and turn it over." Model hand position for the class. "Set one of the claves on top of your fist of this hand; let it rest against your knuckles. Grasp the other clave with the other hand and strike the resting clave." Direct students to demonstrate.

"Tambourines, for this activity, I would like you to tap the tambourine with your free hand, rather than shake the tambourine." Direct students to demonstrate.

Call on the student with the cabasa. Demonstrate how to play the cabasa for the student. "Hold the cabasa by the handle with one hand, and twist it in the palm of your other hand." Direct the student to demonstrate.

Call on the students with the guiros. Demonstrate how to play guiros for students. Scrape the guiro with a wooden pick. "What animal does the guiro sound like when I play?" (a frog) Direct students to demonstrate.

"If you have drums or tambourines, what phrase will you play?" Direct students to the first example. ("Lions and tigers and bears, oh my!") "Yes. Will you play on every word?" (no, only on the beat) "Good! Let me hear you say the phrase and play on the beat." Provide preparatory count. Read the phrase with the students and indicate the beat with your hand. "Great!"

"If you play claves, maracas, or castanets, what phrase will you play?" ("Who's afraid of the big, bad wolf?") "Yes. Let me hear you say this phrase and play on the beat." Provide preparatory count. Read the phrase with the students and indicate the beat with your hand. "Good!"

"If you play guiros, woodblocks, cabasa, and cymbals, you are playing the last phrase. Let's say this phrase together and play on the beat indicated by the red mark." Provide preparatory count. Read the phrase with the students and indicate the beat with your hand. "Good job!"

"Now let's link these phrases so that we have a longer composition. I would like you to say your phrase first and then say it and play it on the repeat. How many times will you say the phrase?" (twice) "Yes. Will you play it the first time?" (no) "You are listening very well! Immediately after phrase one is played, those of you assigned to phrase two need to be ready to say yours. After the second group plays phrase two, the third group will begin by saying its pattern and then playing it. We won't pause between phrases."

"Here we go. Tambourines and drums, let's speak your part and then play it. Eyes on the transparency." Provide preparatory count. Speak with the group. Cue Group 1 to play. Cue Group 2. Speak the second phrase with Group 2. Cue Group 2 to play. Cue Group 3. Speak with Group 3. Cue Group 3 to play. "Excellent job! Let's do this again; this time start softly." Write a "p" over the first phrase on the transparency. "We are going to build the sound as we progress, and by the time we get to the last phrase, we should be speaking and playing loudly." Mark last phrase with an "f" on the transparency. "Remember, Group 1 needs to begin softly so we have somewhere to go with the dynamic level."

"Let's also perform these phrases simultaneously. Group 1 will say its phrase and then repeat it, adding instrumental accompaniment and repeating the phrase, saying and playing it, as I bring in Group 2 and then Group 3. I will cut all of us off together at the end. What will happen to our texture as we add groups?" (It will get thicker.) "Good! What will happen to the dynamic level as we add groups?" (It will get louder.) "Good! Let's not, however, yell at the end."

"Let's try this. Group 1, are you ready?" Provide preparatory count. Speak with the group and cue the repeat. Cue Group 2. Speak with the group and cue the repeat. Cue Group 3. Speak with the group and cue the repeat. Conduct the groups by indicating the beat with your hand until Group 3 has repeated its pattern two more times. Indicate the cutoff for all groups.

## Summary

"Great job! You were watching! Did the dynamic level become louder?" (yes) "Did the texture thicken as groups came in?" (yes) "Do you think an increase in texture will result in an increase in dynamic level?" (yes) "Great playing! May I have different students assist me by collecting instruments?" Choose students. "Thank you for your attention and great efforts today! See you next time!"

# Lesson 17

**Focus**
- Singing a parody song
- Identifying vocabulary words in the context of the song

**Related National Music Standards**
- Grades K–4—Standards 1b, 8b
- Grades 5–8—Standards 1c, 8b

**Materials**
- Transparency—"The Wolf Song"
- Overhead projector

## Introduction

"**G**ood morning! I hope you've had a great week. Who remembers what we did last time?" (We played instruments and read phrases about animals we are studying in reading.) "Great! What word have you been discussing this week that describes information that is used to persuade our thinking, whether it is positively or negatively directed at a cause, a group, or a nation?" (propaganda) "Yes. Today I am going to share with you a song I have created using information that has been presented to you in your reading class. I made up the words, but I borrowed the tune. This is a parody song, because I borrowed another melody to fit my words."

## Process

"How many of you know the song 'My Darling Clementine'?" Students respond. Sing the refrain for the class. "How many of you recognize this song now?" Students raise hands.

"My song uses the melody to 'My Darling Clementine.' Let's look at the words I have written. Let's look at my lyrics to the melody." Display the transparency of "The Wolf Song."

"Let's look first at all of the underlined words. What can you tell me about the underlined words?" (They are types of wolves.) "Yes. Let's read together the first verse about the timber and tundra wolf. Will you read these words to the rhythm

## The Wolf Song
### (Sung to the tune of "My Darling Clementine")

In subarctic wooded regions,
Lives the timber wolf we know.
On the frozen Arctic plains,
Tundra wolves play in the snow.

Once throughout the Southern U.S.,
Red wolves roamed in forests green,
Now endangered and protected,
They are rarely ever seen.

Tales and legends of the wolf
Make our fear of them so great.
Bounty hunters, angry ranchers
Work to stop the wolf they hate.

*In 1987, red wolves were reintroduced into North Carolina. The U.S. government has classified the wolf as an endangered species in every state except Alaska and Minnesota.*

of the melody of 'My Darling Clementine?' I will read aloud with you." Provide preparatory count in simple triple meter. Read the first verse with the class.

"Good! Which wolf lives above the Arctic circle?" (tundra wolf) "Yes. Which wolf would we most likely see in North America?" (timber wolf) "Let's look now at the second verse. Read with me in rhythm." Provide preparatory count. Read the second verse with the class.

"Now let's look at the third verse. We have been discussing propaganda this week. How would tales and legends of the wolf serve as propaganda?" (They create a positive or negative image of the wolf.) "Is the wolf despised today by some people?" (yes) "What measures have hunters and ranchers taken to stop the wolves?" (They have trapped them and poisoned them.) "Correct. Let's read the words to this verse out loud." Provide preparatory count. Read the third verse with the class.

"The paragraph at the bottom of this transparency provides additional information about the preservation of wolves in our country." Call on a student to read the paragraph. "Who can tell me what the word 'reintroduced' means?" (to introduce again) "Yes. If an animal is not released into the wild, but kept caged or housed either in a zoo or a park or even home, what word do we associate with this practice? We say that animal is in what?" (captivity). "Yes. This word is also one of your vocabulary words this week."

"Now, let's sing the entire song. I will bring you in after I count one full measure and two beats." Hum a starting pitch for the class and count them in on the beginning pitch. Sing the song with the class.

"Good job! How does our song differ from 'My Darling Clementine'? What part of our wolf song is missing? Let me give you a clue. We refer to a part of a song that keeps recurring between verses as the what?" (refrain) "Is there a part to 'The Wolf Song' that repeats?" (no) "Does our song then have a refrain?" (no) "No, it does not."

Cover the transparency.

## Summary

"Who remembers what wolf lives in the subarctic?" (timber wolf) "Good. What wolf lives on the Arctic circle?" (tundra wolf) "Yes! What wolf is rarely seen in the southern United States?" (red wolf) "Upon what are our fears of wolves based?" (tales and legends) "What have hunters and ranchers done to try to stop the wolves?" (trapped and poisoned them)

"You have listened closely today. Have a good week!"

# Lesson 18

## Focus
- Singing a parody song
- Creating parody songs based upon the theme of endangered species

## Related National Music Standards
- Grades K–4—Standards 1c, 8b
- Grades 5–8—Standards 1c, 8b

## Materials
- Transparencies—Endangered Animals; Extinct Wildlife; Main Reasons That Species Are Extinct or Endangered; and Song Titles for Compositions
- Overhead projector
- Paper
- Pencils

## Introduction

"Good morning! You will need some notebook paper on your desk today. We are going to be creative! You are going to write your own parody song about an endangered animal of your choice. Before we begin composing, let's sing 'The Wolf Song' from memory!"

Hum starting pitch and cue class to sing. Sing beginnings of phrases and let students complete endings. "Great!"

## Process

"Do you have your paper ready in front of you?" (yes) "Good. Are you ready to create your own song?" (yes) "Here we go! I am going to put some transparencies up on the overhead projector, and I want you to look at the information, decide what you would like to use, and apply that information in your written compositions. Look, decide, apply."

"Here is a list of endangered animals." Display the transparency.

### Endangered Animals

| | |
|---|---|
| Black-footed ferret | Indian elephant |
| Blue whale | Orangutan |
| Burrowing owl | Red wolf |
| California condor | Rhinoceros |
| Cheetah | Ridley sea turtle |
| Crocodile | Snow leopard |
| Galapagos fur seal | Swainson's hawk |
| Great auks (flightless bird) | Tiger |
| Imperial parrot | Whooping crane |

"You won't find every endangered animal on my list, but this list will provide you with some possible choices for your compositions." Read the list aloud to the class. "I obtained this information from your media specialist."

"Here is a list of some extinct wildlife." Display the transparency.

Read the list aloud to the class. Describe those animals unfamiliar to the class. "Choose two animals from these lists to be subjects of your song. You may choose two endangered animals, two extinct animals, or one animal from each list."

"Let's look at some of the reasons these animals are endangered or extinct." Display the third transparency.

"I would like you to include one or two of these reasons in your composition. Perhaps your reasons may explain why the animals you chose for your subjects are endangered or extinct. You may find additional information from the encyclopedias and other materials the media specialist has allowed us to use. Before we go to the encyclopedias, let's look at some songs that are familiar to you." Display the transparency with song titles.

"Let's say the words of 'Are You Sleeping?' while tapping the steady beat." Start the steady beat for the class and cue students to speak. "How are words with more than one syllable broken down to fit the rhythm of the melody?" (They are divided by syllables.) "Who can give me an example of a two-syllable word in this song?" (sleeping, morning, ringing) "Good."

"What kind of sound did we make when we said 'John' and when we said 'dong'?" (a long sound) "Do you see how your words will need to be arranged so that they fit the rhythm of the melody?"

## Extinct Wildlife

California grizzly bear
Carolina parakeet
Dusky seaside sparrow
Giant pied-billed grebe
Little Marianas fruit bat
Palo Verdes blue butterfly
Passenger pigeon

## Main Reasons That Species Are Extinct or Endangered

Agriculture/habitat destruction
Explorers and exploitation
Marine fishing
Wildlife trade
Collecting wildlife
Forest destruction
Industrialization
Pollution
Global warming

## Song Titles for Compositions

Beat grouping of 2
  "Are You Sleeping?"
  "This Old Man"
  "Twinkle, Twinkle, Little Star"
  "Old MacDonald Had a Farm"
  "Over the River and Through the Wood"
Beat grouping of 3
  "On Top of Old Smoky"
  "Down in the Valley"

"You will need to practice saying your words to the tune as you compose them. I will help you if you have problems."

"Let's say the words to 'Twinkle, Twinkle, Little Star.' Tap the steady beat with me as we say them." Start the steady beat for the class. Then speak and tap with the class. "The words you use in your compositions do not have to rhyme. Decide what meter you want to use for your song. Then choose one of the songs on the list in that meter to use as the music for your parody song. If you are fortunate enough to come up with a phrase that describes your animal and the word at the end of the phrase rhymes with another word in your song, that's great! Your composition will be just as original and interesting if you don't have rhyming words."

"I will be glad to help you, and you may help each other, too. We will need to share encyclopedias and materials, especially if some of you choose the same two animals. Be a buddy! Let's get to work!" Monitor students for remainder of lesson. Assist students in locating information and word syllabification if necessary.

## Summary

"Good listening today. I'm looking forward to reading your compositions! Work on them this week and I'll collect them next time. See you then!"

# Lesson 19

## Focus
- Performing a poem expressively
- Accompanying the poem with classroom instruments

## Related National Music Standards
- Grades K–4—Standards 2b, 4a
- Grades 5–8—Standard 8a

## Materials
- Transparency—poem, "Midnight Fox"
- Excerpts from *The Midnight Fox* — in *Invitations to Literacy: Level 5, Explore* (Boston: Houghton Mifflin, 1996); or in Betsy Byars's *The Midnight Fox* (Glenview, IL: Scott Foresman, 1996)
- Instruments—drums, maracas, claves, cabasa, woodblocks, tambourines, xylophone
- Overhead projector

## Introduction

"**G**ood morning! Please open your reading textbooks to page 160. I have been listening to everything being said in your reading class this morning. I heard your discussion of this week's spelling and vocabulary words and their definitions. [Name of student], will you read for us from *The Midnight Fox*? I know your reading teacher has not introduced this story to you, but I want us to read just enough to learn what the story for this week is about. You may begin, [name of student]." Student reads title and author's name. "Oooooh! We know that name! Betsy Byars is on our what?" (spelling list) "Yes! Keep going, [name of student]." Student continues. Assist student reader as needed. "Are there solutions to Tom's problem?" (yes) "You discussed some of them while completing your chart earlier this morning, didn't you?" (yes)

Display the transparency with the poem.

"Ta-dah! We are going to read this together; it is my poem entitled 'Midnight Fox.' My poem is based upon all the information we just heard. [Name of student], read aloud to us on page 160. I have not read the story! I do not know the outcome!"

## Midnight Fox
### (A musical poem based on the book *The Midnight Fox,* by Betsy Byars)

Black fox, midnight fox,
Beautiful fox, desperate fox,
Creeping 'round the farm.

Uncle Fred anxiously awaits her return;
His chickens and turkeys are doomed!
Tom is filled with hopelessness—how can he
protect the fox and her cub?

Black fox, midnight fox,
Beautiful fox, desperate fox,
Creeping 'round the farm.
Creeping 'round the farm.
Creeping 'round the farm.

"We are going to make this a fun poem to read together. Are you ready? Here we go!"

Read the poem with the class. Use vocal inflection, dynamic changes, and appropriate pauses to make the reading more expressive. "Great job! Tom is worried, isn't he?" (yes) "Why?" (because the fox is eating the chickens) "Yes. Do you think he wants to protect the fox?" (yes) "Who does not want to protect the fox?" (his Uncle Fred) "Why is his uncle so anxious? What is the fox capable of doing?" (eating his chickens and turkeys)

"Let's look at the poem again. How many vocabulary words did I use in my poem?" Wait for students' response. "How about the word 'desperate'?" (yes) "Anxiously?" (yes) "Doomed?" (Yes) "Hopelessness?" (yes) "I used four vocabulary words."

Call on students to assist in distributing instruments. "Those of you with woodblocks please raise your hand so that [name of student] knows you need a mallet. Some of these instruments are quiet; that is great. Some of you are allowing them to rest so that you won't lose the privilege of playing them, hint, hint, hint."

"Name of student], you have the cabasa." Demonstrate to student how to play the cabasa. Student demonstrates. "Guess what animal I had in mind for that instrument?" (the fox) "Yes! Where are my maracas players?" (students raise hands) "You represent Tom. Remember, he is worried. When we get to 'Tom is filled with hopelessness,' you shake the maracas. Where are the drums?" Students raise hands. "You represent Uncle Fred. How will you play your drum so that we know that Uncle Fred anxiously awaits the arrival of the fox?" Students tap rapidly on drum heads with finger tips. "Woodblocks and tambourines, we have a lot of you because Uncle Fred has a lot of what?" (chickens and turkeys) "Yes. When we get to the words 'chickens and turkeys,' let us know you are clucking about and rather upset. Claves, you are going to be playing with the xylophone."

"Whoever plays the xylophone will be introducing the poem. I have marked two bars with x's to help you. One of the bars marked with an x will be your starting point. You begin by playing that bar and then a short pattern of your creation as an introduction. We have discussed cadences in music class. Play a melodic pattern on the xylophone that ends on the tonic. Did this pattern sound finished to you? Did the pattern come to a close?" (yes) "What kind of cadence is this?" (a strong cadence) "Yes. To end with a strong cadence, what bar do I need to use as my last pitch?" (one marked with an "x") "Yes. At the end of the poem, do we know what happened to the chickens and the turkeys and the fox?" (no) "So, to end with a question … " Demonstrate on the xylophone. "I did not end my pattern by playing a bar marked with an x. At the end of the poem, will you play a bar marked with an x?" (no)

Remind claves players how to hold their instruments. Model hand position.

"Those of you who do not have instruments, you will play in a few minutes. Help the rest of us by reading the poem very expressively. Let's try this."

"Are you ready? I want instrumentalists to play as we mention your characters and then stop. I'll cue you and cut you off at the right time." Read the poem aloud with the class, cueing instrumental parts.

"After reading 'creeping 'round the farm,' how do you suppose we should end this, softly or loudly?" (softly) Demonstrate on the xylophone. Call on a student who has not played to play the xylophone. Direct students to exchange instruments first with those who have not played.

"Let's play this once again. This time, it would be nice if we could make it a little more musical. Should we start this poem loudly?" (yes) "Why?"

"I don't think I would start it loudly. What kind of animal are we talking about in this poem?" (a fox) "They don't really go around the neighborhood yelling, 'I'm here! I'm here!' " So, it might be a good idea if we start how?" (softly) "Yes, and here is a good clue: 'creeping 'round the farm.' I'm going to put a 'p' here at the beginning to remind us. 'Uncle Fred anxiously awaits her return.' How should we read this phrase?" (loudly) "Loudly. We can be fast here; we're nervous. 'His chickens and turkeys are doomed!' Chickens and turkeys, you really need to let me hear you at this point; you are doomed, your fate is sealed, you are going to be dinner. 'Tom is filled with hopelessness.' What should happen to our dynamic level at the repeat of 'black fox, midnight fox'?" (it should decrease) "Yes. And [name of student] should play even softer as we repeat 'creeping 'round the farm.' " At the very end, the xylophone and claves should be playing extremely softly."

"So here we go. Take two. Let's make this musical. Here we go." Cue xylophone and claves to begin. Cut off and cue class to read. Cue instrumentalists.

## Summary
"Great job! Call on students to collect instruments. You did a wonderful job making this poem expressive! We have used four vocabulary words this morning. I hope discussing them within the context of the poem will help you this week."

"If you have a composition from last time that you would like me to read, please put it on top of your desk and I will collect it. Thanks! See you next time!"

# Lesson 20

**Focus**
- Performing a poem expressively
- Performing excerpts from student parody compositions

**Related National Music Standards**
- Grades K–4—Standard 5a
- Grades 5–8—Standard 5a

**Materials**
- Transparencies—poem, "Midnight Fox" (see Lesson 19); several student compositions; and blanks, for working with student compositions
- Overhead projector

## Introduction

"**G**ood morning! Who remembers what we did last time?" (We sang a song about "Midnight Fox") "We did? Did we sing a song or perform a poem?" (performed a poem) "Yes. Did we talk about the use of dynamics?" (yes) "Is it more interesting if dynamics vary, or change, in our poem?" (yes) "How did we begin the poem, softly or loudly?" (softly) "Yes, and if you remember, I used a 'p' to indicate a soft dynamic level." Write the letter "p" and the term *piano* on the transparency. "Who remembers what letter is used to represent a loud dynamic level?" (an "f") "Good!" Write the term *forte* on the transparency. How could you remember the word *forte* by looking at the letter 'f'?" Wait for student response. "If you take the 'e' off of this word, what do you get?" (fort) "I remember thinking of that word in elementary school. If you were in battle, what would the sound be like coming from a fort?" (loud) "Yes! 'P' for pillow and 'f' for fort; *p* for soft, *f* for loud. Because we found repetition at the end of the poem, what did we decide to do dynamically at the end?" (get softer) "Yes."

"[Name of student], give me one vocabulary word from this poem." (desperate) "What does that mean, [name of student]?" (in much need of, wanting something badly) "Yes. What about the word 'anxiously'?" Wait for students' response. "Suppose I know that I have a test tomorrow, but I have not studied one bit for it. How am I going to feel tonight at home? Calm? Easygoing?" (no) "No! I am going to be worried. I am going to be fretful. I'll be anxious. What about 'doomed'?" (in trouble, in danger) "Tom was filled with ... ?" (hopelessness) "That means what?" (without hope) "Right! He sees no hope for the situation. Let's read the last section of the poem again and remember to read … ?" (softer) "Yes, as you approach the last line." Read with the class.

## Process

"I want to share with you some of the parody compositions you wrote. I realize not everyone turned one in for me to read, but a few of you rose to the occasion and created some wonderful lyrics for your songs. Let's look at these." Display compositions on transparencies.

"Who remembers what meter signature we need to use for 'Are You Sleeping'?" (4/4) "Yes." Write the meter signature on the transparency. Point to the words of the student composition on the transparency. "Let's say this example together." Provide preparatory count in simple quadruple meter.

**Red wolf, red wolf, red wolf, red wolf,**

"Well done! This student made sure that every beat had how many syllables matched to it?" (one) "Yes. Now look at this." Point to two measures of three quarter notes followed by one quarter rest in the student composition on the transparency. "Let's read aloud the words beneath these patterns. Clap the pattern with me." Provide preparatory count.

**Where are you? Where are you?**

"Let's look at the next phrase." Point to the third phrase on the transparency. "Read these words with me." Provide preparatory count.

**You live in the U.S., You live in the U.S.,**

"Do these words fit the pattern ti-ti-ti-ti ta, ti-ti-ti-ti ta?" (yes) "They do!"

"And, after all of this, we end with a rhyming phrase! Read aloud with me." Provide preparatory count.

**Yes, you do. Yes, you do.**

"Excellent job, [name of student]! Let's read this once again. Here we go!" Provide preparatory count. Read with the class.

"Another example." Display another student composition and point to the transparency. "Read with me."

**Where are cheetahs? Where are cheetahs?**

"Good. Look at the next phrase." Point to the second phrase.

**In Africa, in Africa,**

"Watch what I do to this so that you see how this can fit." Hyphenate the word "Africa" beneath a pair of eighth notes and a quarter note. "Do you notice in your music book that words are hyphenated below notes so that the syllables fit the rhythmic pattern?"

Point to the third phrase. "Read this phrase with me in rhythm." Provide preparatory count.

**They're the fastest mammals, they're the fastest mammals**

"Do these words fit the rhythm of 'morning bells are ringing, morning bells are ringing'?" (yes) "They do!"

"Remember the last phrase of 'Are You Sleeping'?" ("ding, ding, dong") "Yes. Let's look at this phrase."

**That live on earth, that live on earth.**

"How many syllables are there in 'that live on earth'?" (four) "How many notes do we have sounding here?" (three) Call on a student. "Can we do something to one of the quarter notes?" (make two eighth notes) "Yes. We will use a beam to connect them." Draw two eighth notes and connect them with a beam on the transparency. "Now we have a pattern that allows us to say 'that live on earth'! Good job, [name of student]!"

Display the transparency with another student composition. "We are going to look at just one part of this example." Write out notation of four eighth notes and two quarter notes on a transparency and display it. "We are going to clap it together." Provide preparatory count.

"Someone came up with this and I helped out the student." Write out words on the transparency.

**Are endangered, are endangered**

"This time, instead of having too many syllables, we did not have enough. So we need to extend the 'Are' and the 'en' syllable of endangered. Listen to me first and then clap and say the pattern with me using the words." Demonstrate for the class. Cue the class to repeat.

"Here is another example using the same rhythmic pattern." Write out words on a transparency and display it.

**Whales and cheetahs, whales and cheetahs**

"What will we have to do to the words 'whales' and 'and'?" (extend them by using a dash underneath the second eighth note in each pair) "Do you see how the syllables of the words need to fit the rhythmic pattern?" (yes)

## Summary

"Thank you for your hard work and creative efforts! These compositions are wonderful. Your reading teacher has told me that you have a few minutes to work before break. Make the most of your time!"

# Related Research

Integrated instruction has been a topic of discussion for educators, researchers, and curriculum specialists for several decades. Advocates of integrated instruction argue that students can learn to transform knowledge into personally useful tools in order to learn new information and to avoid the fragmented and irrelevant acquisition of isolated facts.[1] The following review of literature includes descriptions of studies related to music as a facilitator of nonmusic learning, as well of summaries of research findings concerning the integration of music into language arts curricula. In educational curricula, communication skills, such as reading comprehension and vocabulary, are defined as components of language arts. Additionally, studies regarding factors that affect both reading achievement and attitude, and music achievement and attitude are reviewed. This review of research is included here to provide music and reading teachers with information regarding music instruction as a tool for learning in other areas of the curriculum.

## Nonmusic Outcomes of Music Education

The success of integrated instruction, in part, depends upon students' transfer of learning from one discipline to another. Transfer of learning has been the focus of research by psychologists and educators for over one hundred years.[2] Bruner believed that "learning should not only take us somewhere; it should allow us later to go further more easily."[3] This belief serves as a premise upon which transfer of learning is based. Tunks defined transfer of learning as

> the effect of learning skills, knowledges, or attitudes on the later learning of other skills, knowledges, or attitudes. Learning transfer also includes the application of learned skills, knowledges, or attitudes in novel settings.[4]

Transfer of learning across cognitive, psychomotor, and affective domains is virtually ignored in the literature; however, investigations of nonmusic outcomes of music learning are plentiful in music education research. Although numerous studies on the transfer of music learning to other subject areas appear in music education research, Wolff indicated that conclusions drawn from this research generally remain unconvincing due to weaknesses in experimental treatments and designs, and the lack of collaboration between educators from other subject areas and music educators.[5] Wolff explained that "definitive evidence of the nonmusic outcomes of music education is yet to be provided."[6] The study for which the lessons in *Integrating Music and Reading Instruction* were developed was designed to maximize integration of reading and music learning via the collaboration of reading and music educators.

One way music has been used to facilitate nonmusic learning is as a reward for accomplishing a task. Madsen has conducted extensive research on using music as a reinforcer for nonmusic behavioral change. Madsen and Forsythe examined the effect of contingent music listening on correct mathematical responses.[7] Subjects for this study were eighty-eight sixth-grade students who were assigned to four groups. Two groups received "popular listening" and two received "dance-listening" as rewards for correct mathematical responses. Results of the one-week experiment revealed that contingent music listening increased correct responses to mathematical problems. However, effects of the music contingencies on correct math responses were not significantly different. Madsen, Dorow, Moore, and Womble also investigated the effects of contingent music activities on developing mathematical skills.[8] Televised music lessons were used as a reward for first-grade students who responded correctly to mathematical problems. Results of this study demonstrated increased math achievement for the group viewing televised music lessons.

Madsen conducted another study to compare the differential effects of receiving televised music lessons and books as reinforcements for third-grade students' achievements in math.[9] The study was based on an extended reversal design over a six-week period. A baseline was established across the first week of the experiment; alternating book and music contingencies were offered the five remaining weeks. During book-contingency weeks, subjects received tokens that could be exchanged for books of their choice. During the music-contingency weeks, subjects received tokens that could be exchanged for televised music lessons. Prior to baseline sessions, all subjects had been assigned to appropriate academic tasks by their classroom teacher. Results of the study showed that both reinforcers increased students' math achievement; however, televised music lessons appeared to facilitate students' maintenance of correct math responses while books did not.

Hallequist examined the integration of music learning into a sixth-grade class about the geography of Germany.[10] Within this study one geography class received integrated music and geography instruction, and another class did not receive integrated instruction. Results showed that integrated music and geography instruction did not significantly increase students' retention of knowledge about Germany's geography. Immediately after treatment, however, the integrated music and geography class achieved higher Germany geography test scores than the nonintegrated class.

Background music in the learning environment facilitates a variety of educational activities such as creative writing, mathematical computing, handwriting, spelling, and drawing and painting.[11] Background music in the learning environment helps relax learners, minimizes distractions, and stimulates thinking. In a reading class, research showed that the aural environment often influences the way students process what they read.[12] Mullikin and Henk conducted a study to measure the reading performance of forty-five subjects in grades four through eight after they were exposed to a variety of auditory backgrounds.[13] Subjects who experienced a classical music background while reading comprehended more than subjects who experienced a rock music background and than subjects experiencing no music background. Subjects who experienced no music background, however, retained more than subjects who experienced either a classical or rock music background. Varied auditory backgrounds during reading differentially affect reading comprehension. For most subjects, rock music should not be used as an auditory background; however, a classical music background facilitates increased reading comprehension.

Smith and Davidson examined the effects of varied music and no music backgrounds on seventh-grade subjects' natural science achievements.[14] Within the study, subjects were divided into four groups that were differentiated by rock, classical, easy listening, and no music backgrounds. While studying the earth-sun relationship during the natural science class individually, subjects experienced one of the four auditory backgrounds. The researchers found that there were no significant differences among students who studied while experiencing either rock, classical, easy listening, or no music background.

## Integrated Reading and Music Instruction in Language Arts Curricula

Communication skills, specifically reading skills and attitudes, are considered to be components of language arts in educational curricula. Music and education researchers have suggested that there is a positive relationship between music and language arts instruction and learning. Walters theorized that music and language arts have parallel skill development areas.[15] For example, listening, speaking, reading, and writing skills that students develop in the context of language arts instruction also are developed in the context of music instruction. McDonald concurred with Walters and explained that music instruction can be used to develop various language arts skills, such as auditory discrimination, word pronunciation, and vocabulary expansion.[16] Monroe identified three basic similarities between music and language reading, including aural-visual discrimination, left to right eye-coordination, and music and language vocabulary retention.[17] She developed a sequence of integrated reading and music lessons based upon these commonalities. Based upon theories of music and language arts learning, integrating music into reading instruction provided students opportunities to develop skills and attitudes common to both subject areas from different content perspectives. Empirical research on integrated reading and music instruction is minimal. Additionally during the past three decades, investigations of integrated instruction generally have produced disparate findings.

Movsesian studied the transfer of music reading skills to developing first-, second-, and third-grade students' vocabulary, reading comprehension, and oral reading skills.[18] Pretests and posttests included the *California Achievement Test,* a researcher-designed *Survey of Primary Music Reading Development,* and the *Gray Oral Reading Test.* Results of the study indicated that experimental subjects in the first, second, and third grades increased more than the control subjects across each test. When specific music skills were taught, Movsesian found that first- and second-grade students improved their basic skills with the exception of oral reading skills. Additionally, first-grade students' reading comprehension increased as a result of concurrent music-reading instruction, as did second-grade students' vocabulary and reading comprehension.

Lauder investigated the effects of integrated reading and music instruction on first-grade students' vocabulary and reading comprehension as measured by the *California Tests of Basic Skills* (CTBS).[19] Both groups received music instruction taught by a music teacher. In addition to music instruction, the experimental group received integrated reading and music instruction. Integrated instruction included: (a) music exercises correlated with vocabulary and reading comprehension, (b) music experiences focused on aural-visual discrimination of words and on vocabulary expansion, and (c) oral reading of song lyrics. Results showed no significant differences between the experimental and control groups' scores on the CTBS vocabulary and reading comprehension subtests. Unlike the Movsesian study,[20] Lauder found no corollary outcome of integrated reading and music instruction relative to reading achievement.

Turnipseed investigated effects of classical music listening instruction on auditory discrimination skills of first-grade students.[21] Subjects in the experimental group participated in classical music listening instruction; whereas, the control group received no music listening instruction. Results indicated that students in the experimental group as compared to the control group scored higher on reading and language arts tests and achieved higher scores on an auditory discrimination skills test. Additionally, as secondary outcomes of the experimental treatment, Turnipseed observed that experimental subjects increased their abilities to be original and flexible during creative activities, received higher grades in reading and mathematics, and missed fewer days of school when compared to the control subjects.

Colwell investigated the effect of shared reading paired with music instruction on kindergarten children's reading accuracy.[22] The kindergarten class participated in a whole language approach. This approach evolved from the pedagogical ideas of John Dewey during the first half of the twentieth century and was based upon the theory that reading and writing are forms of language and function like other forms of language. During the past twenty years, the whole language movement has influenced reading education, particularly in the primary grades.[23]

In the 1994 Colwell study, shared reading was a core activity in the classroom that involved teacher and student participation. The teacher read text while pointing to the words. Students responded by reading when able, supplying isolated words left off by the teacher, and answering questions about the text. The music program was implemented by a music therapist. The therapist met with each of the three classes for twenty minutes, two days per week for twelve weeks. In addition to integrating music into the whole language curriculum, the purpose of implementing the music program was to determine the effect of shared reading paired with music on subjects' reading accuracy. One of three shared reading treatment conditions was assigned to each group including: (a) song rehearsal of text set to music, (b) spoken and song rehearsal of the text set to music, and (c) spoken rehearsal only of the text. Results of the study showed that the song rehearsal of text set to music, and the spoken and song rehearsal of text set to music, yielded significantly greater accuracy during shared reading responses by students than spoken rehearsal only of text.

Research on integrated reading and music instruction in language arts curricula has produced applicable and practical outcomes. Results from several studies showed that singing and studying song lyrics help students link oral and written language by analyzing rhyme, rhythm, and repetition of vocabulary terms and within story structures.[24] These researchers also concurred that songs serve as structural prompts to reinforce the relationship between song-text and book-text meanings. In a review of research on the use of song lyrics and singing to facilitate reading skills, Whitaker suggested that when music specialists carefully select song materials, students are provided numerous opportunities to develop reading skills through the combination of moving, reading, writing, and creating activities.[25] Research on integrated instruction showed that several common reading and music concepts, such as meter, rhythm, accent, and form, may be explored. Additionally, the research supported using musical instruments to augment the dramatization of stories and poems.

## Factors Affecting Reading Achievement and Reading Attitude

Numerous studies have shown that there is a relationship between reading ability and reading attitude.[26] One factor that may confound research findings relative to reading achievement and attitudes is gender. Research has shown that gender is an important factor to consider when investigating elementary children's reading achievement and reading attitudes.

Generally, research studies demonstrated that girls tend to have more positive attitudes toward reading than boys.[27] Mullis, Campbell, and Farstrup found that females establish and maintain an early advantage in reading ability.[28] McKenna suggested that gender-based advantages in reading ability may positively affect females' attitudes toward reading.[29] In McKenna's research, females consistently demonstrated more positive attitudes than males. McKenna theorized that, as compared to males, females are more likely to believe they will have successful reading experiences.

From a national sample of fourth-, eighth-, and twelfth-grade students, Williams found that female subjects continued to score higher in reading achievement than male subjects across all three grade levels compared to reading achievement scores obtained from a 1992 sample.[30] Han and Hoover, using nationally standardized test scores from 1963 to 1992, examined the effect of gender and grade level on students' performances on the *Iowa Tests of Basic Skills, Iowa Tests of Educational Development,* and the *Tests of Achievement and Proficiency.*[31] The researchers found that female subjects scored higher than males in reading and language skills, and in mathematical computation, up to age fifteen. Additionally, females' verbal tests scores were higher than males' scores in the upper grade levels.

Effects of gender and past music learning experiences on reading achievement also have been investigated. Dryden examined the effect of instrumental music instruction on the academic achievement of 270 fifth-grade students.[32] Results of the study showed that band students' reading vocabulary and total reading achievement scores were higher than scores of students not enrolled in instrumental instruction. Dryden also found that male subjects who received instrumental instruction increased in reading vocabulary. Results of research suggest that both music background and gender affect fifth-grade students' reading achievement and attitudes. Research on the effects of integrated reading and music instruction on reading achievement and reading attitude, therefore, should control for the possible confounding effects of gender and music background.

## Factors Affecting Music Achievement and Music Attitude

Both gender and music background have been found to be factors influencing music achievement and music attitude. Students' attitudes toward music instruction may vary according to gender.[33] Pogonowski found that fifth-grade girls exhibited the highest global music attitude, or "cumulative effect of subjective associations [which] students develop toward music."[34] She concluded that both grade level and gender are significant predictors of music attitudes. Additionally, she found low positive relationships among music attitudes, private instrumental study, and performing group membership. These relationships suggest that classroom music attitudes generally were not related to subjects' participation in band, chorus, orchestra, or private music study.

Mizener examined the attitudes of elementary music students toward singing and choir participation.[35] Grade level, gender, classroom singing activities, past and present out-of-school singing experiences, and degree of singing skill were considered relative to attitudes toward music. Most of the third- through sixth-grade subjects indicated a positive attitude toward singing, although less than half expressed interest in choral singing. The most positive responses were elicited from girls, younger students, those who enjoyed singing, and those who wanted to sing in a choir. Results of the study suggested that music specialists should plan activities to strengthen and support positive associations with music experiences. Furthermore, girls and younger children expressed positive perceptions of their singing when encouraged by their parents. Mizener recommended the implementation of programs of family education in the schools that stress the importance of positive parental attitudes toward music in developing children's music attitudes.

Numerous research studies support the theory that positive attitudes toward school music activities decline with each advancing grade at the elementary level.[36] In the study for which the lessons in *Integrating Music and Reading Instruction* were developed, grade level was kept constant by using only fifth-grade students. Research also has shown that at all grade levels, girls generally have more positive attitudes toward music than boys.[37] Other factors associated with music attitude include playing instruments, out-of-school music experiences, self-concept, and self-esteem.[38] To control for the possible differential effects of gender and music background on music achievement and attitude, indicators of these variables were obtained and examined.

The research reported in this chapter includes findings about nonmusic outcomes of music learning and about integrated reading and music instruction in language arts curricula. Integrating music into language arts to improve reading skills and develop students' reading abilities is supported. Effects of integrated reading and music instruction using children's literature on students' reading and music achievements and attitudes, however, have not been demonstrated empirically. Additionally, research findings showed that gender and music background may affect students' reading and music achievements attitudes; therefore, research on integrated reading and music instruction must control for these potentially confounding variables.

## Notes

1. M. Y. Lipson, S. W. Valencia, K. K. Wixson, C. W. Peters, "Integrating and Thematic Teaching: Integration to Improve Teaching and Learning," *Language Arts* 70 (1993), 252–63.

2. Thomas W. Tunks, "The Transfer of Music Learning," in *Handbook of Research on Music Teaching and Learning,* edited by Richard Colwell, 437–47 (New York: Schirmer, 1992).

3. J. Bruner. *The Process of Education* (Cambridge: Harvard University Press, 1960), 17.

4. Tunks, 437.

5. K. L. Wolff, "The Nonmusical Outcomes of Music Education: A Review of the Literature, *Bulletin of the Council for Research in Music Education* 55 (1977), 1–27.

6. Wolff, 21.

7. Clifford K. Madsen and Jere L. Forsythe, "Effect of Contingent Music Listening on Increases of Mathematical Responses," *Journal of Research in Music Education* 21, no. 2 (1973), 176–81.

8. Clifford K. Madsen, Laura G. Dorow, Randall S. Moore, and Jeana U. Womble, "Effect of Music via Television as Reinforcement for Correct Mathematics," *Journal of Research in Music Education* 24, no. 2 (1976), 51–59.

9. Clifford K. Madsen, "Music Lessons and Books as Reinforcement Alternatives for an Academic Task," *Journal of Research in Music Education* 29, no. 2 (1981), 103–110.

10. R. Hallequist, "An Experimental Study Correlating Music with the Teaching of Geography in the Sixth Grade," doctoral diss., University of Mississippi, 1968.

11. G. Cohen-Taylor, "Music in Language Arts Instruction," *Language Arts* 58, no. 3 (1980), 363–67 (ERIC/RCS report); and M. L. Greenhoe "Parameters of Creativity in Music Education: An Exploratory Study," doctoral diss., University of Tennessee, 1968.

12. R. F. Carey, J. C. Harste, and S. L. Smith, "Contextual Constraints and Discourse Processes: A Replication Study," *Reading Research Quarterly,* 16, no. 2 (1981) 201–212.

13. C. N. Mulliken and W. A. Henk, "Using Music as a Background for Reading: An Exploratory Study," *Journal of Reading* 28 (1985) 353–58.

14. B. A. Smith and C. W. Davidson, "Music and Achievement," *Journal of Social Studies Research* 15, no. 1 (1991), 1–7.

15. Darrel L. Walters, "Sequencing for Effective Learning," in *Handbook of Research in Music Teaching and Learning,* edited by Richard Colwell, 535–45 (New York: Schirmer, 1992).

16. D. McDonald, "Music and Reading Readiness," *Language Arts* 52 (1975), 872.

17. M. E. Monroe, "A Study of Music Reading in Elementary School Utilizing Certain Related Aspects of Language Reading," doctoral diss. Columbia University, 1967.

18. E. A. Movsesian, "The Influence of Teaching Music Reading Skills on the Development of Basic Reading Skills in the Primary Grades," doctoral diss., University of Southern California, 1967.

19. D. C. Lauder, "An Experimental Study of the Effect of Musical Activities upon Reading Achievement of First-Grade Students," doctoral diss., The University of South Carolina, 1976 (*Dissertation Abstracts International* 37, 1975A).

20. Movsesian.

21. J. P. Turnipseed, "The Effect of Participation in Structured Classical Music Education Program on the Total Development of First-Grade Children," paper presented at the Mid-South Educational Research Conference, 1976.

22. C. M. Colwell, "Therapeutic Applications of Music in the Whole Language Kindergarten," *Journal of Music Therapy* 31 (1994), 238–47.

23. S. A. Stahl, M. C. McKenna, and J. R. Pagnucco, "The Effects of Whole Language Instruction: An Update and Reappraisal," *Educational Psychologist* 29 (1994), 175–85.

24. K. Dulaney-Barclay and A. Coffman, "Lyrical Literacy," *Teaching K–8* (1990), 57–59; K. Dulaney-Barclay and L. Walwer, "Linking Lyrics and Literacy through Song Picture Books," *Young Children* 47 (1992), 76–85; and C. Wiseman, "Singing the Book," *Book Links* (1992), 56–59.

25. Nancy Whitaker, "Whole Language and Music Education," *Music Educators Journal* 81 (July 1994), 24–28.

26. M. A. Anderson, N. A. Tollefson, and E. C. Gilbert, "Giftedness and Reading: A Cross-Sectional View of Differences in Reading Attitudes and Behaviors," *Gifted Child Quarterly* 29 (1985), 186–89; J. A. Lipsky, "A Picture-Story Technique to Uncover Covert Attitudes Associated with Reading Failure," *Reading Psychology* 4 (1983), 151–55; C. E. Martin, "Why Some Gifted Children Do Not Like to Read," *Roeper Review* 7 (1984), 72–75; and H. J. Walberg and S. Tsai, "Correlates of Reading Achievement and Attitude: A National Assessment Study," *Journal of Educational Research* 78 (1985), 159–67.

27. Anderson, Tollefson, and Gilbert; E. P. Ross and R. K. Fletcher, "Responses to Children's Literature by Environment, Grade Level, and Sex," *Reading Instructional Journal* 32 (1989), 22–28; M. C. Smith, "A Longitudinal Investigation of Reading Attitude Development from Childhood to Adulthood," *Journal of Educational Research* 83 (1990), 215–19; and H. W. Stevenson and R. S. Newman, "Long-Term Prediction of Achievement and Attitude in Mathematics and Reading," *Child Development* 57 (1986), 646–57.

28. I. V. S. Mullis, J. R. Campbell, and A. E. Farstrup, *NAEP 1992: Reading Report Card for the Nation and the States* (Washington, D.C: U.S. Department of Education, 1993).

29. M. C. McKenna, " Toward a Model of Reading Attitude Acquisition," in *Fostering the Love of Reading: The Affective Domain in Reading Instruction*, edited by E. H. Cramer and M. Castle (Newark, DE: International Reading Association, 1994), 18–40.

30. P. Williams, *1994 NAEP Reading: A First Look—Findings from the National Assessment of Educational Progress* (Princeton, NJ: Educational Testing Service, 1995).

31. L. Han and H. D. Hoover, "Gender Differences in Achievement Test Scores," paper presented at the annual meeting of the National Council on Measurement in Education, New Orleans, Louisiana, 1994.

32. S. Dryden, "The Impact of Instrumental Music Instruction on the Academic Achievement of Fifth-Grade Students," master's thesis, Fort Hays State University, 1992.

33. Patricia E. Sink, "Research on Teaching Junior High and Middle School General Music," in *Handbook of Research in Music Teaching and Learning,* edited by Richard Colwell (New York: Schirmer, 1992), 602–612.

34. Lenore M. Pogonowski, "Attitude Assessment of Upper Elementary Students in a Process-Oriented Curriculum," *Journal of Research in Music Education,* 33, no. 4 (1985), 247–58.

35. Charlotte P. Mizener, "Attitudes of Children toward Singing and Choir Participation and Assessed Singing Skill," *Journal of Research in Music Education* 41, no. 3 (1993), 233–45.

36. T. Haladayna and G. Thomas, "The Attitudes of Elementary School Children toward School and Subject Matters," *Journal of Experimental Education* 48 (1979), 18–23; Donald K. Taebel and Joan G. Coker, "Teaching Effectiveness in Elementary Classroom Music: Relationships among Competency Measures, Pupil Product Measures, and Certain Attribute Variables," *Journal of Research in Music Education* 28, no. 4 (1980), 250–64; and S. D. Vander Ark, W. H. Nolin, and I. Newman, "Relationships between Musical Attitudes, Self-Esteem, Social Status, and Grade Level of Elementary Children," *Bulletin of the Council for Research in Music Education* 62 (1980), 31–41.

37. R. D. Crowther and K. Durkin, "Sex- and Age-Related Differences in the Musical Behaviour, Interests, and Attitudes towards Music of 232 Secondary School Students," *Educational Studies* 8 (1982), 31–139; and Vander Ark, W. Nolin, and Newman.

38. Manny Brand, "Relationship between Home Musical Environment and Selected Musical Attributes of Second-Grade Children," *Journal of Research in Music Education* 34, no. 2 (1986), 111–120; O. H. Broquist, "A Survey of the Attitudes of 2594 Wisconsin Elementary School Pupils toward Their Learning Experience in Music," doctoral diss. University of Wisconsin, Madison, 1961 (*Dissertation Abstracts International* 22, 1917A); W. E. Mawbey, "Wastage from Instrumental Classes in Schools," *Psychology of Music* 1 (1973), 33–43; Mary Kotts Murphy and Thomas S. Brown, "A Comparison of Preferences for Instructional Objectives between Teachers and Students," *Journal of Research in Music Education* 34, no. 2 (1986), 134–39; W. H. Nolin and S. D. Vander Ark, "A Pilot Study of Patterns of Attitudes toward School Music Experiences, Self-Esteem and Socio-Economic Status in Elementary and Junior High Students," *Contributions to Music Education* 5 (1977), 31–46; and J. N. Svengalis, "Music Attitude and the Preadolescent Male," doctoral diss., University of Iowa, Iowa City, 1978 (*Dissertation Abstracts International* 39, 4800A).

# Grades K–4 National Standards for Music Education

## 1. CONTENT STANDARD: Singing, alone and with others, a varied repertoire of music
### Achievement Standards:

Students

    a. sing independently, on pitch and in rhythm, with appropriate timbre, diction, and posture, and maintain a steady tempo

    b. sing expressively, with appropriate dynamics, phrasing, and interpretation

    c. sing from memory a varied repertoire of songs representing genres and styles from diverse cultures

    d. sing ostinatos, partner songs, and rounds

    e. sing in groups, blending vocal timbres, matching dynamic levels, and responding to the cues of a conductor

## 2. CONTENT STANDARD: Performing on instruments, alone and with others, a varied repertoire of music
### Achievement Standards:

Students

    a. perform on pitch, in rhythm, with appropriate dynamics and timbre, and maintain a steady tempo

    b. perform easy rhythmic, melodic, and chordal patterns accurately and independently on rhythmic, melodic, and harmonic classroom instruments

    c. perform expressively a varied repertoire of music representing diverse genres and styles

    d. echo short rhythms and melodic patterns

    e. perform in groups, blending instrumental timbres, matching dynamic levels, and responding to the cues of a conductor

    f. perform independent instrumental parts while other students sing or play contrasting parts

### 3. CONTENT STANDARD: Improvising melodies, variations, and accompaniments
*Achievement Standards:*

Students

    a. improvise "answers" in the same style to given rhythmic and melodic phrases

    b. improvise simple rhythmic and melodic ostinato accompaniments

    c. improvise simple rhythmic variations and simple melodic embellishments on familiar melodies

    d. improvise short songs and instrumental pieces, using a variety of sound sources, including traditional sounds, nontraditional sounds available in the classroom, body sounds, and sounds produced by electronic means

### 4. CONTENT STANDARD: Composing and arranging music within specified guidelines
*Achievement Standards:*

Students

    a. create and arrange music to accompany readings or dramatizations

    b. create and arrange short songs and instrumental pieces within specified guidelines

    c. use a variety of sound sources when composing

### 5. CONTENT STANDARD: Reading and notating music
*Achievement Standards:*

Students

    a. read whole, half, dotted half, quarter, and eighth notes and rests in 2/4, 3/4, and 4/4 meter signatures

    b. use a system (that is, syllables, numbers, or letters) to read simple pitch notation in the treble clef in major keys

    c. identify symbols and traditional terms referring to dynamics, tempo, and articulation and interpret them correctly when performing

    d. use standard symbols to notate meter, rhythm, pitch, and dynamics in simple patterns presented by the teacher

### 6. CONTENT STANDARD: Listening to, analyzing, and describing music
*Achievement Standards:*

Students

    a. identify simple music forms when presented aurally

    b. demonstrate perceptual skills by moving, by answering questions about, and by describing aural examples of music of various styles representing diverse cultures

    c. use appropriate terminology in explaining music, music notation, music instruments and voices, and music performances

    d. identify the sounds of a variety of instruments, including many orchestra and band instruments, and instruments from various cultures, as well as children's voices and male and female adult voices

e.  respond through purposeful movement to selected prominent music characteristics or to specific music events while listening to music

## 7. CONTENT STANDARD: Evaluating music and music performances
### *Achievement Standards:*
Students

a.  devise criteria for evaluating performances and compositions
b.  explain, using appropriate music terminology, their personal preferences for specific musical works and styles

## 8. CONTENT STANDARD: Understanding relationships between music, the other arts, and disciplines outside the arts
### *Achievement Standards:*
Students

a.  identify similarities and differences in the meanings of common terms used in the various arts
b.  identify ways in which the principles and subject matter of other disciplines taught in the school are interrelated with those of music

## 9. CONTENT STANDARD: Understanding music in relation to history and culture
### *Achievement Standards:*
Students

a.  identify by genre or style aural examples of music from various historical periods and cultures
b.  describe in simple terms how elements of music are used in music examples from various cultures of the world
c.  identify various uses of music in their daily experiences and describe characteristics that make certain music suitable for each use
d.  identify and describe roles of musicians in various music settings and cultures
e.  demonstrate audience behavior appropriate for the context and style of music performed

# Grades 5–8
# National Standards for
# Music Education

## 1. CONTENT STANDARD: Singing, alone and with others, a varied repertoire of music
### Achievement Standards:

Students

    a. sing accurately and with good breath control throughout their singing ranges, alone and in small and large ensembles

    b. sing with expression and technical accuracy a repertoire of vocal literature with a level of difficulty of 2, on a scale of 1 to 6, including some songs performed from memory

    c. sing music representing diverse genres and cultures, with expression appropriate for the work being performed

    d. sing music written in two and three parts

Students who participate in a choral ensemble

    e. sing with expression and technical accuracy a varied repertoire of vocal literature with a level of difficulty of 3, on a scale of 1 to 6, including some songs performed from memory

## 2. CONTENT STANDARD: Performing on instruments, alone and with others, a varied repertoire of music
### Achievement Standards:

Students

    a. perform on at least one instrument accurately and independently, alone and in small and large ensembles, with good posture, good playing position, and good breath, bow, or stick control

    b. perform with expression and technical accuracy on at least one string, wind, percussion, or classroom instrument a repertoire of instrumental literature with a level of difficulty of 2, on a scale of 1 to 6

c. perform music representing diverse genres and cultures, with expression appropriate for the work being performed

d. play by ear simple melodies on a melodic instrument and simple accompaniments on a harmonic instrument

Students who participate in an instrumental ensemble or class

e. perform with expression and technical accuracy a varied repertoire of instrumental literature with a level of difficulty of 3, on a scale of 1 to 6, including some solos performed from memory

## 3. CONTENT STANDARD: Improvising melodies, variations, and accompaniments
### *Achievement Standards:*
Students

a. improvise simple harmonic accompaniments

b. improvise melodic embellishments and simple rhythmic and melodic variations on given pentatonic melodies and melodies in major keys

c. improvise short melodies, unaccompanied and over given rhythmic accompaniments, each in a consistent style, meter, and tonality

## 4. CONTENT STANDARD: Composing and arranging music within specified guidelines
### *Achievement Standards:*
Students

a. compose short pieces within specified guidelines, demonstrating how the elements of music are used to achieve unity and variety, tension and release, and balance

b. arrange simple pieces for voices or instruments other than those for which the pieces were written

c. use a variety of traditional and nontraditional sound sources and electronic media when composing and arranging

## 5. CONTENT STANDARD: Reading and notating music
### *Achievement Standards:*
Students

a. read whole, half, quarter, eighth, sixteenth, and dotted notes and rests in 2/4, 3/4, 4/4, 6/8, 3/8, and alla breve meter signatures

b. read at sight simple melodies in both the treble and bass clefs

c. identify and define standard notation symbols for pitch, rhythm, dynamics, tempo, articulation, and expression

d. use standard notation to record their musical ideas and the musical ideas of others

Students who participate in a choral or instrumental ensemble or class

e. sightread, accurately and expressively, music with a level of difficulty of 2, on a scale of 1 to 6

## 6. CONTENT STANDARD: Listening to, analyzing, and describing music
### Achievement Standards:

Students

    a.  describe specific music events in a given aural example, using appropriate terminology

    b.  analyze the uses of elements of music in aural examples representing diverse genres and cultures

    c.  demonstrate knowledge of the basic principles of meter, rhythm, tonality, intervals, chords, and harmonic progressions in their analyses of music

## 7. CONTENT STANDARD: Evaluating music and music performances
### Achievement Standards:

Students

    a.  develop criteria for evaluating the quality and effectiveness of music performances and compositions and apply the criteria in their personal listening and performing

    b.  evaluate the quality and effectiveness of their own and others' performances, compositions, arrangements, and improvisations by applying specific criteria appropriate for the style of the music and offer constructive suggestions for improvement

## 8. CONTENT STANDARD: Understanding relationships between music, the other arts, and disciplines outside the arts
### Achievement Standards:

Students

    a.  compare in two or more arts how the characteristic materials of each art (that is, sound in music, visual stimuli in art, movement in dance, human interrelationships in theatre) can be used to transform similar events, scenes, emotions, or ideas into works of art

    b.  describe ways in which the principles and subject matter of other disciplines taught in the school are interrelated with those of music

## 9. CONTENT STANDARD: Understanding music in relation to history and culture
### Achievement Standards:

Students

    a.  describe distinguishing characteristics of representative music genres and styles from a variety of cultures

    b.  classify by genre and style (and, if applicable, by historical period, composer, and title) a varied body of exemplary (that is, high-quality and characteristic) musical works and explain the characteristics that cause each work to be considered exemplary

    c.  compare, in several cultures of the world, functions music serves, roles of musicians, and conditions under which music is typically performed

## Level of Difficulty

For purposes of these standards, music is classified into six levels of difficulty:

*Level 1*—Very easy. Easy keys, meters, and rhythms; limited ranges.

*Level 2*—Easy. May include changes of tempo, key, and meter; modest ranges.

*Level 3*—Moderately easy. Contains moderate technical demands, expanded ranges, and varied interpretive requirements.

*Level 4*—Moderately difficult. Requires well-developed technical skills, attention to phrasing and interpretation, and ability to perform various meters and rhythms in a variety of keys.

*Level 5*—Difficult. Requires advanced technical and interpretive skills; contains key signatures with numerous sharps or flats, unusual meters, complex rhythms, subtle dynamic requirements.

*Level 6*—Very difficult. Suitable for musically mature students of exceptional competence.

(Adapted with permission from *NYSSMA Manual,* Edition XXIII, published by the New York State School Music Association, 1991.)

# Selected Resources

## Children's Literature Used in the Lessons in This Book

Byars, Betsy. *The Midnight Fox*. Glenview, IL: Scott Foresman, 1996.

Freedman, Russell. *Children of the Wild West*. New York: Clarion Books, 1983.

Freedman, Russell. *Buffalo Hunt*. New York: Holiday House, 1988.

Freedman, Russell. *Cowboys of the Wild West*. New York: Clarion Books, 1985.

Freedman, Russell. *Indian Chiefs*. New York: Holiday House, 1987.

Freedman, Russell. *Lincoln: A Photobiography*. New York: Clarion Books, 1987.

Gleeson, Brian. *Pecos Bill*. Narrated by Robin Williams. New York: Rabbit Ears/Simon & Schuster, 1997. Book and CD.

Lester, Julius. *John Henry*. New York: Dial Books, 1994.

Stein, R. Conrad. *The Story of the Oregon Trail*. Chicago: Children's Press, 1984.

Tichenor, John. "Pecos Bill." *In Invitations to Literacy: Level 5, Explore,* edited by J. D. Cooper and J. J. Pikulski. Boston: Houghton Mifflin, 1996.

Voight, Erna. *Peter and the Wolf*. Adapted from Prokofiev. Boston: David R. Godine, 1980.

## Music Used in the Lessons in This Book

*World of Music*. Grade 5. Parsippany, NJ: Silver Burdett Ginn, 1988, 1991.

*Making Music*. Grade 5. Glenview, IL: Silver Burdett/Scott Foresman, 2002.

*The Music Connection*. Grade 5. Parsippany, NJ: Silver Burdett Ginn, 1995.

*Share the Music*. Grade 5. New York: Macmillan/McGraw-Hill, 1995, 2000.

## Recorded Music Used in the Lessons in This Book

(*Note:* This music is in addition to the recordings referenced from the basal series listed above.)

Chopin, Frederic. "Fantasie-Impromptu in C# minor," op. 66.

Copland, Aaron. *Lincoln Portrait*.

Grofé, Ferde, "Sunrise." *Grand Canyon Suite*.

Prokofiev, Sergei. *Peter and the Wolf*.

Vaughan Williams, Ralph. "Fantasy on a Theme by Thomas Tallis."

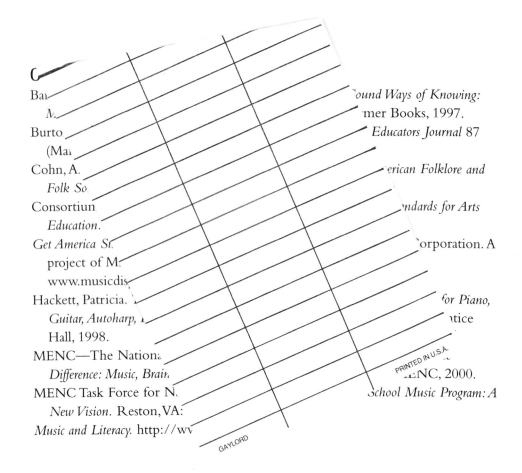

Bar... ...ound Ways of Knowing: ...mer Books, 1997.

Burto... ...Educators Journal 87

(Mar...

Cohn, A. ...erican Folklore and

Folk So...

Consortium... ...ndards for Arts

Education.

Get America St... ...orporation. A

project of M...

www.musicdis...

Hackett, Patricia. ...for Piano,

Guitar, Autoharp, ... ...tice

Hall, 1998.

MENC—The National ...

Difference: Music, Brain... ...NC, 2000.

MENC Task Force for N... School Music Program: A

New Vision. Reston, VA:

Music and Literacy. http://ww...